The Pope's Wedding

The Pope's Wedding was given its first production at the Royal Court Theatre in 1962 and was Edward Bond's first play to be staged. It is about Scopey, a young East Anglian farm worker and his marriage to Pat, a village girl who has inherited an obligation to look after Alen, an old hermit who lives in a corrugated iron hut outside the village. Gradually Scopey becomes obsessed with the old man and this involvement brings about his downfall. Scopey's strange history unfolds in a sharply authentic context of life amongst the village boys with its limited horizons. *The Pope's Wedding* is a strikingly original play that looks forward to Bond's subsequent achievement in *Saved*. This volume also includes the sketch *Black Mass* and a number of recent prose and verse pieces.

The photograph on the front of the cover shows a scene from the production by the Rose Bruford College at the Arts Theatre, London in 1970 and is reproduced by courtesy of Peter Theobald; the photograph on the back of the cover is reproduced by courtesy of Mark Gerson.

by the same author

SAVED
NARROW ROAD TO THE DEEP NORTH
EARLY MORNING

The Pope's Wedding

EDWARD BOND

METHUEN & CO LTD
11 NEW FETTER LANE · LONDON EC4

This volume first published 1971 by Methuen & Co Ltd
'The Pope's Wedding' Copyright © 1969 by Edward Bond
'Mr Dog' and 'Sharpeville Sequence' © 1970 by Edward Bond
'The King With Golden Eyes' © 1971 by Edward Bond

Printed in Great Britain by
Cox & Wyman Ltd., Fakenham, Norfolk
SBN 416 08870 8 (hardback edition)
SBN 416 09210 1 (paperback edition)

Contents

The Pope's Wedding

THE POPE'S WEDDING was first performed at the Royal Court Theatre on Sunday December 9th 1962 with the following cast:

SCOPEY, twenty-two	Philip Lowrie
BILL, twenty-four	David Ellison
RON, twenty	Michael Standing
LEN*, seventeen	
LORRY, eighteen	Malcolm Patton
JOE, twenty-one	Malcolm Taylor
BYO, twenty	Lawrence Craine
ALEN, seventy-five	Harold Goodwin
PAT, eighteen	Janie Booth
JUNE, sixteen	Adrienne Hill
BOWLER	Julian Chagrin
WICKET KEEPER	George Ogilvie
UMPIRE (heard but not seen)	

Directed by Keith Johnstone

* Excluded from the original production.

BILL and BYO are big-boned and muscular. LEN and SCOPEY are a bit shorter. LORRY is the smallest. JOE is a bit fat. JUNE whitens her face and heavily paints her eyebrows and lashes. She is small and thin. PAT is quite short, but she has heavy shoulders and a very full figure. Her bright country complexion shows through her cosmetics.

In these sixteen scenes the stage is dark and bare to the wings and back. Places are indicated by a few objects and these objects are described in the text. The objects are very real, but there must be no attempt to create the illusion of a 'real scene'. In the later scenes the stage may be lighter and Scene Fifteen may be played in bright light.

Scene One

An open space. An iron railing up stage centre. This is used for
leaning against.

SCOPEY, BILL, RON, LEN, LORRY, JOE, BYO.

BILL *forces* SCOPEY's *head under his left armpit.* SCOPEY *is bent*
double from the waist.

SCOPEY. Lego. Lemeegoo!

BILL. 'Ow's that for an arse, boy?

> *He hits* SCOPEY's *arse with his right hand.* SCOPEY *hits him in*
> *the kidneys with his right fist.*

Ow! Bastard!

SCOPEY. I 'ope that'll teach yoo a lesson.

BILL. Bastard!

SCOPEY. Next time yoo keep yoor 'ands a yoorself.

BILL. Yoo owd pook – yoo got the money rightnough.

RON. 'Oo's got the time?

LORRY. Gettin on.

BYO. Must be.

JOE. Been fast all day.

BYO. What?

JOE. My watch.

BYO. Put her right.

RON. 'Ow can 'e, 'e ent got the time.

LORRY. Gettin on.

BILL. To me.

BYO. To yoo. (*He kicks a stone.*)

JOE. To me.

BILL. To yoo.

RON. To me.

JOE. To yoo.

BILL. To me. Let's 'ave it.

RON. To yoo. Wake up. (*Kicks the stone to* SCOPEY.)

SCOPEY. Owzat!

JOE. Well stopped.

SCOPEY (*kicks*). Goal!

BILL. 'Oo's settin' the beer up?

 SCOPEY *groans*.

RON. On a Thursday?

LORRY. Syoor turn I reckon, ent it?

BILL. Well lend us the money an' I'll treat the lot on yer.

LORRY. That's a rum owd doo, me lendin' yoo money to pay for
my own beer.

BILL. Yoo'll get it back.

LEN. Yoo 'ope.

LORRY. Don't worry, I ent lendin' it. I ent got it

BILL. No beer? No beer.

 Pause.

BYO. Bleep bleep.

BILL. Yoo got a licence for that, boy?

 Pause.

BILL. Come on, Sco. Five bob.

SCOPEY. I seen yoo back a Farrin field sarternoon.

BILL. I was 'idin' up from owd man Bullright's woman. Anyone
out on the road a see yoo down there, so she 'as t' lay off.

JOE. That's a rum owd doo, ent it, 'avin' the boss's missis come
after yer.

BYO. Yoo keep in there, boy. Yoo stan' a doo yoorself a bit a
good.

LORRY. I reckon 'e's leadin' 'er on.

BILL. She don't need no leadin', boy. My life!

JOE. 'Er owd man'll cop 'er one day.

LEN. I'd like a see that.

BILL. Shut up.

 Pause.

RON. Light up the vicarage.

BILL. God workin' overtime.

JOE. Yoor mouth.

BILL. Let's goo an' burn a yank.

BYO. Bloody work tmorra.

JOE. Yoo wouldn't know what a doo with yoorself if it wasn't.

BYO. I'd know what a doo with yoo.

BILL. Five bob. Four bob. Two an' six. One bent shillin'.

SCOPEY. Put it on the slate.

BILL. I tried that yesterday.

JOE. Got a smoke?

BILL. Chriss, I'd sell my sister if I 'ad one.

LORRY. Yoo thirsty?

LEN. If she was anythin' like yoo t'ent likely yoo get much for 'er.

BILL. 'Op it. Oi, I saw that Butty girl bendin' down in 'er yard when I come by. Neigh come off my bike.

BYO. Yoo like it fat.

BILL. Soft, mate, soft.

SCOPEY. Where they come from?

BILL. Saw right up 'er arse. Chriss – where's that beer?

SCOPEY. Why she bendin' down?

BYO. That owd stone tore my boot.

BILL. This week I reckon I'll stow a few bottles under that owd stairs while I still got the dough.

SCOPEY. That won't be there be Monday.

RON. Lights off up the vicarage.

BILL. Now 'e's showin' 'is missis the second comin'. They're all the same in the dark.

SCOPEY. What?

BILL. 'Ow old yoo reckon that Butty girl is?

RON. Seventeen.

BYO. Big ginger crutch.

Pause.

JOE. I saw.

BILL (*not hearing*). What?

JOE. I saw.

BYO. Not agen?

LORRY. Me?

JOE. I saw it.

LORRY. Yeh?

JOE. I saw all right. Yoo thought I ent lookin'.

LORRY. Me?

JOE. Yoo know.

BILL. No beer?

LORRY. 'Onest a God I never –

JOE. Yoo thought I wasn't lookin', didn't yoo. I was lookin' right enough. I saw.

LORRY. 'Oo cares?

JOE. Yoo will, boy.

BYO. Yoo gooin' a make 'im?

JOE. Yeh.

BYO. Goo on then. .

JOE. What yoo puttin' in for?

BYO. Let's see yoo.

JOE. I was watchin'.

LORRY. My arse.

JOE. I got eyes in my 'ead.

LORRY. Yoo want a use 'em.

JOE. I use 'em all right.

LORRY. Yoo weren't even lookin'.

JOE. No?

LORRY. No.

BILL. Wrap up.

RON. 'Ent yoo gooin' a fight?

BYO. They couldn't 'it a fly on the end a their nose.

JOE. Just let me catch yoo next time an' you'll know it.

LORRY. Yeh?

JOE. Yoo try.

BILL. 'Ent yoo got a few bob. They're drivin' me nuts.

JOE. Little sod.

BILL. 'Alfa crown an' I'll share me crisps.

RON. I oiled that owd Ferguson this mornin'. Yoo should a seen
    'er. My life!

LORRY. They don't know ow t' look after proper gear.

JOE. 'Oo asked yoo?

LORRY. 'Oo asked yoo?

BYO. For Chriss sake fight it out, yes?

LORRY. Eh?

RON. Fight it out, for Chriss sake.

JOE. 'Oo asked yoo what t' doo?

RON. Well that's – obvious – fight it out.

BYO (*to* JOE). Don't yoo want a 'it 'im?

LORRY. 'E started it.

JOE. I'll 'it 'im anytime. I'll 'it anyone.

BILL. Just carry me down to the Carpenter's Arms.

    Slight pause.

LEN. Five tmorra.

    Pause.

RON. Yoo got a light, boy?

BILL. Yup.

BYO. Ow about a smoke? Ta.

RON. That's three yoo owe me.

BYO. Three? I give yoo two last Wednesday.

RON. Wednesday?

BYO. Wednesday, when yoo come up agen owd Pete's place.

RON. O, long a owd Pete's. That come back now.

BYO. That make one.

RON. That come back now.

    Pause.

BYO. Yoo seen them new shirts they got out?

SCOPEY. Where?

BYO. They got round collars.

RON. That's been out a long time.

BYO. I ent see it. Reckon I'll buy one a them.

BILL. Borrow yoor owd dad's.

BYO. Saucy sod.

Hits BILL *on the ear. They fight.*

BILL. Fix 'im, Sco. Use yoor boot.

BYO. Yoo try.

SCOPEY. Cut it out. (*He parts them.*)

BYO (*to* SCOPEY). That 'urt, boy.

PAT *and* JUNE *come in down right.*

BILL. Lend us five bob.

PAT. On a Thursday?

BILL. Yoo broke?

PAT. I was gooin' a ask yoo t' buy me some fags.

BILL. Shouldn't smoke.

PAT. Lot I shouldn't doo by rights.

BILL. No one wants t' see yoo perfect.

PAT. No? (*To* BOY). 'Ello.

BYO. Comin' 'ome with me?

JUNE. 'Fraid a the dark?

BYO. I like someone t' owd my 'and.

PAT. I bet.

BILL. Didn't yoor owd boy Alen give yoo nothin'.

PAT. Yoo know 'e don't pay me.

BILL. For 'is shoppin'.

PAT. I ent touchin' that.

BILL. Just till tmorra. I'll give yoo back.

PAT. T'ent mine t' lend.

BILL. 'E won't know.

PAT. I ent gooin' a give 'im the chance.

JOE *laughs.*

JUNE. Yoo takin' somethin' for that?

BILL. Just till tmorra.

PAT. No.

BILL. I'll leave it with yoor gran on my way 'ome from work.

PAT (*to* JUNE). Comin'.

BILL. They'll be closed in 'alf an 'our.

PAT. T'ent worth gooin'.

BILL. Time for a quick one.

JUNE (*to* PAT). Come on.

BYO (*to* BILL). She treat yoo like owd dut, boy. Yoo want a put yoor foot down.

JUNE. On yoo.

BILL. Suppose I kick yoor 'ead in an take yoor purse.

PAT. Wouldn't be worth the bother, boy.

BILL. 'Alf a crown.

JOE. Tuppence.

LEN. Brew yoor own.

    JOE *laughs.*

JUNE. 'E's off agen.

PAT. 'Ave a cup of tea. Doo yoo more good.

JOE (*laughing*). 'Er owd mum's beetroot wine!

JUNE. Dial 999.

JOE (*laughing*). That'll rot yoor owd gut.

PAT. What's wrong with 'im?

BILL. Toss yoo 'alf a crown.

    SCOPEY *lifts* PAT's *skirt as she passes him.*

SCOPEY. They're white.

PAT (*shrilly amused*). Yoo owd devil! Lemmee goo! Yoo see that? 'E lifted it right up! Yoo wicked owd devil! They're white!

BYO. I reckon that for a pair a top legs.

PAT. Yoo wicked owd sauce! Yoo ent better doo that a Mrs Bullrights. She don't wear none, 'cordin' a owd Bill.

JUNE. What d'ee doo?

PAT. Lucky I 'ad mine on! Cheeky owd devil!

JUNE. What d'ee do?

PAT. 'E saw my (*spells*) n-i-c-k-s! (*Very amused.*) They're white! (*To* BOYS.) Did yoo see? (*To* BYO.) Did yoo see?

    SCOPEY *snatches her bag.*

Yoo let that be!

He throws it to BYO.

That's new. I just 'ad that.

B

RON. To me.

> BYO *throws it to him.*

LORRY & JOE. To me.

RON. To yoo. (*Throws it to* LORRY.)

LORRY. To yoo. (*Throws it to* BILL.)

SCOPEY. To me.

PAT. I got that a goo with my new shoes.

JUNE (*to* PAT). Stay there. I'll catch him. (*She goes to* SCOPEY.)

BILL. To yoo. (*Throws it to* BYO.)

LEN. To me.

BYO. To yoo. (*Throws it to* LEN.)

PAT. Yoo sods!

JOE. To me. (*He catches it.*) That's yoors. (*Throws it to* SCOPEY.)

> JUNE *gets one hand on it.*

PAT. 'Old it. (*She runs to* SCOPEY *and tugs at the bag.*) Give me! (*The strap breaks.*) O!

SCOPEY. Too yoo. (SCOPEY *throws it to* RON.)

JUNE. Yoo broke it.

RON. To yoo. (*Throws it to* LEN.)

PAT. Yoo sods! Yoo sods! Yoo rotten sods!

> LEN *holds it. He is unsure what to do.*

Yoo rotten stinkin' bastards.

BILL (*to* LEN). Let her 'ave it.

JUNE. Rotten bastards, now look what yoo done.

LEN. Catch. (*Throws it to* PAT.)

PAT. Rotten bastards. That's my new bag.

JUNE. She got that a goo with 'er new shoes. Sods. Is that spoilt, gal?

PAT. 'Course it's spoilt!

JUNE (*to* SCOPEY). Yoo started that.

PAT. Rotten sod.

JUNE. 'E's the worst one.

PAT. Rotten little sod.

JUNE. Yes.

PAT. Yoo're pay for a new one.

SCOPEY. Don't sod me!

BILL. Well what yoo want a doo that for?

BYO. Twot.

SCOPEY. I was only larkin'.

BILL. Larkin'!

SCOPEY. Yoo 'elped.

BILL. 'Oo started?

JUNE. Yes.

PAT. That's no good a me. June (*she takes handfuls of things from her bag*) take that. Put that in yoor pocket gal, (*She takes a hanky from the bag and wipes her eyes.*)

JUNE. Sods. Now yoo upset 'er.

PAT. Their great dirty 'ands all over. (*She puts the last of her things in her pocket. She throws the bag to* SCOPEY.) Now yoo buy a new one.

SCOPEY. I ent buyin' nothin'.

PAT. Yoo pay up or I come round yoor 'ouse.

JUNE. An' me.

SCOPEY. Goo where yoo like. Yoo shouldn't a got a cheap owd one in the first place. That won't stand up t' proper 'andlin'.

PAT. I didn't ask for one for yoo t' kick about.

JUNE. Yoo won't think that's cheap when yoo see the bill.

SCOPEY. You know where yoo can stick the bloody bill.

PAT. You'll pay, don't worry. Bastards.

    PAT *and* JUNE *go out left.*

BYO. Don't she get worked up.

BILL. I 'ont gooin a get no loan off 'er tonight.

BYO. See what yoo *can* get.

    Pause. RON *lights a cigarette and hands one to* BYO.

LEN. Thank God it's nigh on weekend.

BILL. Yoo ought a be in bed.

JOE. Chriss that's close. (*He wipes his neck.*) I been sweatin' like a pig.

SCOPEY. That owed strap pulled off the 'ook, that's all. That ent torn n' nothin'. I can easy fix that. It weren't on right for the first place. She never give much for that, doo they robbed 'er. That could be a pulled off when she were out shoppin', then she'd a been slummocksed. (*Takes a piece of paper from the bag.*) Owd ticket. (*Sniffs it.*) Powder. (*Sniffs.*) Mauve. (*Throws it away.*) Just push the strap back on a nip with the owd pliers. Doo that afore I goo t' bed, easy.

RON. Up in seven hours.

BILL. I'd best goo an' see 'ow she's gettin' on.

BYO. Don't forget a put somethin' on the end a it.

BILL. Thanks for the tip.

LORRY & RON. 'Night.

BILL. See yoo tmorra.

RON. In the saloon, mate.

BILL. Early. 'Night.

SCOPEY & JOE. 'Night.

BYO. 'Night, boy.

> BILL *goes out Left.*
> *Pause.*
> SCOPEY *swings the bag on the strap.*

Scene Two

An apple on the stage.
SCOPEY, BILL, RON, LORRY, JOE.
They each carry a scythe.
RON. Short back and sides.

> JOE *holds* LORRY. BYO *moves the scythe blade over the back of* LORRY'S *head.*

BYO. Ha! I got some! (*He pulls some hairs from* LORRY'S *head.*)

LORRY. I'll smash yoo, boy!

JOE. Watch out!

BYO. Duck's arse.

LORRY. When I get out!

BILL. Ent yoo mob workin'?

LORRY. First time I 'eard yoo want a work. Ow!

BILL. I ent 'angin' round 'ere all day mate.

LORRY. Get these bastards off an' we'll start.

> *They let him go.*

   Try that agen!

> JOE *laughs.*

BYO. Do'n'ee look cross.

LORRY. I'll maim yoo one day.

BILL. One little guzzle an' I'm ready. (*He takes half a pint of brown ale from his trouser pocket.*)

SCOPEY. 'Oo yoo pinch that off?

JOE. I got sweat muck all over me.

SCOPEY. Where yoo pinch that?

BILL. I can smell yoo from 'ere. Goo down wind, boy. Move.

BYO. Me an' Bill'll doo under the trees an' yoo lot take the sides atween yer.

SCOPEY. What's Joe dooin'?

BILL. 'Elpin' yoo.

LORRY. Oo's got the fags afore we start?

RON. Where's yoorn?

LORRY. I give mine out this mornin'.

SCOPEY. Not when I was there.

JOE. Yoo what?

LORRY. Don't bother.

JOE. I ent.

BILL (*to* BYO). Yes?

BYO. Ta. (BYO *takes the bottle. He drinks.*)

RON. Pig.

BYO. Lovely.

LORRY (*to* RON). Ent yoo got no fags?

BILL. Up! (*He swings his scythe in a circle.*)

> LORRY *and* SCOPEY *have to jump.*

   Yoo ent got a leg to stand on as the copper said when the burglar came round on the operatin' table.

SCOPEY. Bloody nut.

JOE. Teach yoo t' jump.

SCOPEY. More 'andy t' duck.

BYO. Finish 'er off. (*He hands the bottle back to* BILL.)

LORRY. Borrow yoor paper? (*Takes paper from* BILL's *jacket.*)
Want t' see what I fancy for this afternoon.

BILL. Oo's layin' ten bob next Saturday?

RON. No thanks.

BILL. Come on, won't bet on yoor own side?

LORRY. I'll believe it when I see it. They thrashed us three times
in the last four year.

RON. We ent got no good bowlers. That's where we fall down.

BILL. We ent never 'ad a battin' side like we got this year afore.
I reckon we could pull it off.

JOE. That's all a question of luck, anyroad.

RON. Cricket ent luck. That's strength and skill and guts.

BILL. Right. (*Sits.*)

SCOPEY. Thought yoo was gooin' a work.

BILL. Must let the beer goo down.

SCOPEY. I knew that wouldn't last.

BILL. Let it settle.

SCOPEY. I never 'ad none.

LORRY. 'Ard luck.

LORRY, JOE, BYO *and* RON *sit.* BYO *picks up the apple. He eats.*
Pause.

SCOPEY. Up yoo.
Pause.

BYO. Right up.
Pause.

LORRY. They win this year they keep the plack.

BILL. They still got owd man Bullrights. Yoo ent got no one a send
'em down alf fasts 'e doo, 'is time a life –

SCOPEY. No?

BILL. – an' I don't reckon yoo ever will 'ave.

SCOPEY. 'E won't be playin' next year.

BYO. 'E will.

SCOPEY. But I don't reckon 'e'll be captain after this.

BILL. 'E don't even practise. Goo out there year after year an' find perfect length first ball.

LORRY (*wiping scythe blade*). Beautiful owd thing, ent she. 'Ung 'er up in owd apple tree t' take the rust out on 'er.
(*Sings.*) Betty drop your drawers it's Monday
No I dropped my drawers on Sunday.

LEN (*sings*). I'm gooin' a pull them off for yoo
I'll cut yoor tail off if yoo doo.

BILL. Anytime.

BYO. Join the queue.
Pause.

RON. Owd Tanner Lob's gooin', then.

LORRY. Cancer all over.

SCOPEY. I 'erd it got 'is lungs.

JOE. Up 'is pipe.

RON. Runnin' all over.

BILL. On the brain.

LORRY. 'E won't be 'arvestin' this year.

RON. Ready?

BILL. No.

LORRY. Fair owd day, ent it.

BYO. It got 'im in the groin.

RON. Yoo got it in the groin.

BYO. I got somethin'.

BILL. Doo it grow?

BYO. Only when yoo're around.
LEN *comes in up left.*

LEN. Mum's chasin' yoo.

BILL. Let 'er.

LEN. She's roarin' for that wringer.

BILL. Yoo fix it for 'er.

LEN. That's yoor job.

BILL. She can wait.

LEN. Yoo ent 'eard 'er roarin'.

BILL. I 'eard 'er all last night on her bloody wringer.

BYO. Ent yoo stand up to 'er yet?

BILL. I just kicked 'er teeth out, kneed 'er in the crutch, set light to 'er 'air, an' she died beggin' me t' forgive 'er.

LORRY. Did yoo?

BILL. No.

LORRY. Got a cigarette?

LEN. No.

BILL. 'E wouldn't give yoo the pickings off 'is arse.

LEN. Yoo comin'?

BILL. No.

JOE. 'E's 'elpin' us. Yoo tell 'er if we don't tidy this place up today we 'ont never get no chance afore the match.

BILL. That's 'er fault anyroad. She 'ont used that wringer right since the day she got it. She wrestle with it.

LORRY (*to* LEN). Yoo smoke?

BILL. 'E's too bloody mean, boy. Oi, gimp howd a that an' make yoorself 'andy. (*He pokes his scythe at* LEN.)

LEN. Yoo ent playin' Saturday.

BILL. No?

LEN. Mum say –

BILL. O yeh? Why?

LEN. Owd man Bullright's been tellin' 'er –

BILL. She can't stop me.

SCOPEY. What's 'e say?

LEN. 'E say if 'e goo off next Saturday 'e'll 'ave t' 'ave someone stayed on the farm.

SCOPEY. That's count a 'is owd red poll.

LORRY. She ent still sick?

BILL. Why me?

LEN. 'E ent got no one for 'andlin' animals barrin' yoo, so 'e say.

BILL. Foxy owd sod.

BYO. Bastard.

BILL. That's rotten play, ent it?

SCOPEY. Can 'e doo it?

BILL. 'E can afford to.

RON. 'E ent takin' no chances this year. That's 'is last year for captain an' 'e's out a keep 'is owd plack.

LORRY. We been playin' for that must be sixty year.

BILL. Bastard.

JOE. Say no.

BILL. With that spiteful owd sod?

SCOPEY. Why not?

BILL. There's plenty waitin' for my job, boy.

JOE. Well that's us finished.

BILL. The sod. (*Twists his scythe.*) I'd like t' 'ave 'is owd 'ead stuck on this.

BYO. Twelfth man in then.

RON. I ent laid that bet.

SCOPEY. I'll doo some trainin'.

BYO. Yoo need to.

JOE. Can't 'e get someone in from outside?

BYO. Don't be bloody daft –

BILL. That's just what 'e don't want a doo, ent it.

   Pause.

   LORRY *practises imaginary off-breaks.*

LORRY. I reckon owd Alen's put 'is curse on us. Owzat! Our owd telly broke down last Wednesday an' the old owd man reckon that's count a 'e cursed us on mum tellin' 'alf the village about Sarah Neat's baby. Owzat!

BILL. Bastard! I'll poison 'is bloody cow. I'll bloody well lay 'is missis for a start. I'll grind 'er, for one. 'E can stick 'is bloody plack but I'll bloody well thread 'is missis.

RON. Supposin' we practise 'ard an' we win the toss or it belts down, we could keep 'em out till it's too late for 'em t' doo much, with a bit a luck.

LORRY. Cricket's a game a skill an' guts an' that.

RON. That ent cricket.

LEN. Owd Sco can howd a catch, anyway.

BILL. Pity 'e can't howd a bat or bowl.

LORRY. Owzat.

BYO. They can't be feelin' too sure a 'emselves, doo they'd never play dirty like that.

RON. That's a fact.

Scene Three

ALEN's *place.*

Across the stage a black and purple corrugated iron wall. A door centre. A couch right. A table down left. Two oil cookers standing on a box down right. Two wooden boxes used as chairs. A stack of newspapers, one foot high, against the wall, right of the door. Three or four smaller stacks of newspapers about the room.

ALEN *alone.*

He stands by the door. He is rigid. He listens. He goes to the table. He goes farther down left. He takes a paper from the floor. He goes to the wall and places the paper on the stack. He goes back down left. Stoops to pick up a paper. Stops. Starts to read. His mouth moves. He slowly withdraws into himself. Wanders aimlessly right. Stops. Listens. Listens more intently. Half turns to the door. Clutches paper. Pause. His attention slowly goes back to the paper. He reads. He goes to the table and spreads the paper on it. He is reading all the time. Stops reading, goes down left, picks up paper, takes it to the wall and places it on the stack. Steps back. Steps forward on to the stack. Pause. Steps down. Wanders aimlessly to the cookers.

Goes back to the table and reads the paper on it. Pause. Scratches chin. Picks up the paper. Goes down left, still reading. Picks up a second paper and goes up right, still reading the first paper. Before he reaches the stack he drops the second paper. Pause. Goes down left and stoops to pick up a third paper, still reading the first paper. Abruptly halts, bent. Listens briefly. Picks up the third paper, still carefully listening. Goes up right. Stops when he reaches the second paper. Looks down at it. Pause. Picks it up. Takes it to the table. Goes up right,

*reading first paper. Places third paper on stack. Steps back. Steps
forward on to stack. With his back to the audience he places his ear
against the wall. He listens. Pause. He steps down. He goes to the
table. He picks up the second paper. He turns and starts to go back to
the wall. Stops. Goes back to the table. Places second paper on table.
Starts to pull table towards wall. Almost immediately a tin falls from
the table on to the floor. Stops. Picks up the tin. Puts it on the table.
Places first paper on a box behind him. Places both palms on the edge
of the table and makes a small effort to raise himself. Gives it up. Sits
on the box. Stands. Takes first paper from box. Sits. Pause. Stands.
Places first paper on box. Goes to the table. Takes second paper from
table and places it on the floor by the table. Stands on second paper
and places both palms on the table as before. Pause. Makes no effort
to raise himself. Steps off second paper. Picks it up. Puts it on the
table. Takes first paper from the box. Reads.*
A bang on the door.
ALEN (*a sigh – gasp.*)

Scene Four

Empty stage.
LORRY *runs in from the right. He is dressed completely in white and
carries a cricket bat. He groans. He follows the high flight of a ball
with his eyes.*
VOICES (*off*). Owzat!
> LORRY *shrugs and walks down right. Clapping. He meets*
> SCOPEY *as he comes on down right.*
LORRY. Whew! 'E's movin' owd Tanner in t' silly mid on.
SCOPEY. Tryin' to get me rattled.
LORRY (*irritated*). Never mind that. Yoo watch out.
SCOPEY. Yoo did all right.
LORRY. I never 'ad no support. Forty t' get. Don't give me a
chance.
SCOPEY. Yoo knock a couple off, boy.

LORRY. They're comin' down like sputniks. I reckon 'e's out t'
knacker yer.

SCOPEY. I'll be –

LORRY. Yoo got a get thirty-two. Yoo 'ont never get thirty-two,
but owd Joe's good for a dozen. Then that 'ont look like they
used us for a mat.

SCOPEY. 'E won't get one if 'e don't come out after 'em –

LORRY. Yoo let 'im play 'is own game. Now don't yoo forget, 'e'll
'it that second ball an yoo run –

SCOPEY. They're waitin'.

LORRY. – like 'ell.

> LORRY *goes out down right.* SCOPEY *takes up his position left
> centre.* BOWLER *runs in from left and bowls.* SCOPEY *stiffens.
> Pause.* BOWLER *catches ball as it is fielded back to him. He walks
> off left. Pause.* BOWLER *runs in from left and bowls.*

SCOPEY. Yes!

> SCOPEY *runs out right.*

> JOE *runs in right and touches into crease.*

SCOPEY (*off*). Yes!

JOE. No! No! CHRISS!

> SCOPEY *runs in from the right.*

JOE. No!

> JOE *dashes out right.* SCOPEY *touches into the crease. Shouts off
> stage.* SCOPEY *wipes his forehead with a handkerchief. Pause.
> He looks round at the field. He takes up his position. His heels
> are three inches apart. His right foot is parallel with the crease.
> His left foot points to cover. His chest and shoulders are square to
> point. His knees are relaxed. His weight is evenly balanced. His
> head is upright and his eyes are level. He alerts. He plays the
> first ball forward on to the pitch. Pause. Hooks the second ball
> past deep fine leg.*

JOE (*off*). Yes!

> SCOPEY *runs off right and* JOE *runs in right. He touches into the
> crease.*

SCOPEY (*off*). Yes!

JOE. No!

>SCOPEY *runs in from the right.*

JOE. Bloody fool.

>JOE *runs out right.* SCOPEY *touches into crease. He takes up his stance. Suddenly he drives the ball past forward short leg. Applause. Shouts of 'Six!' Pause.* SCOPEY *settles into his stance again. He suddenly cuts to cover. Loud applause. Shouts of 'Four'. Settles into his stance. Moves out and hits a straight drive. Loud applause. Shouts of 'Six!' Pause. Suddenly he tries to glance the ball to leg. Hastily twists to look behind him and touch into his crease. Onlookers groan. Silence. Loud clapping.* JOE *comes in jerkily from the right.* SCOPEY *goes to meet him.*

JOE. For Chriss sake goo easy!

SCOPEY. What?

JOE. Eighteen in one over! Yoo're takin' chances. Twelve t' win! Yoo 'ont a take them chances, boy, we can't afford it. Goo steady an' let me 'ave a crack. Yoo 'ad yoor turn a luck but that 'ont never last a second time.

>JOE *goes out right.* SCOPEY *returns to his crease.* BOWLER *runs in from the left and bowls. He catches the returned ball and spins to face* SCOPEY. SCOPEY *is in his crease.* BOWLER *goes out left, throwing the ball a few feet in the air and catching it.* BOWLER *runs in from left. He bowls. It is a short ball.*

BOWLER AND OTHER VOICES. Owzat!

UMPIRE (*off stage*). No ball.

>*Murmurs.* SCOPEY *looks down at his feet, bending swiftly from the waist.* BOWLER *wipes the back of his neck. He catches the returned ball and goes out left, throwing it and catching the ball with one hand. He runs in from left and bowls. A second passes and the* BOWLER *leaps forward into the air, snatches for the ball, falls forward, his left knee giving way. He lies with his back to the audience. Stands. Tugs at his belt, scoops up the ball – which has landed a few feet in front of him. Goes out left, gripping the ball. Pause. Runs in from left. Bowls. Applause. He catches the returned ball. He goes off left. He runs in. He bowls.*

JOE (*off*). Yes!

SCOPEY. No! No!

> BOWLER *whips up the returned ball. Spins to face* SCOPEY.
> BOWLER *starts to go left.*

BOWLER (*with a dry spit*). Last 'un.

> BOWLER *goes out left. Runs in. Bowls. Applause.* SCOPEY *runs
> out right and passes* JOE *as he runs in.* JOE *reaches the crease.*

SCOPEY (*off*). Yes!

JOE. No! Sco!

> SCOPEY *runs in from right.* JOE *runs out right. Applause.* JOE
> *comes in from right.* SCOPEY *strolls a few steps to meet him.*

JOE. Ten! We could doo that. We got to, Chriss! Doo we'll never
'ear the last on it. Yoo all right? Goo easy. 'Ow yoo doin'?

SCOPEY. All right.

JOE. Chriss, yoo 'ont better try nothin' fancy this time. (*Wipes his
forehead.*) Chriss, I'm that 'ot!

SCOPEY. They're ready, Joe.

JOE. 'E's pushed owd Tanner cross t' deep square leg. Goo steady.
Chriss, I know somethin'll come a balls it up.

> JOE *goes out right.* SCOPEY *settles into his crease. Pause. He
> glances the ball elegantly to leg. Shouts of 'Four!' And loud
> applause. He suddenly flinches. Onlookers groan. Pause, and*
> SCOPEY *slowly swings his bat from side to side. Stops. Looks
> round at the field – first and second slips, gully, mid off, forward
> short leg, deep fine leg, deep backward square leg, cover point and
> third man. Alerts. Suddenly dashes down the field and smashes
> the ball past mid on.*

SCOPEY. YES! YES! YES!

> SCOPEY *runs out right.* JOE *runs in right.*

JOE (*running*). God! I can't stand it!

SCOPEY (*off*). YES! YES! YES!

JOE. That voice! (*He drops his bat.*) Aaaaahhhh God!

> SCOPEY *runs in from the right.*

SCOPEY (*running*). YES! YES! YES!

> JOE *whinnies. Snatches up his bat. Dashes right.*

JOE (*running*). FOUR MORE! FOUR MORE!

SCOPEY. YES! YES! YES!

JOE *runs out right. The onlookers are in an uproar.* SCOPEY *looks patiently down the pitch. Alerts. Leaps forward. Swoops on the ball. The bat cracks. The ball smashes past mid on. Shouts of 'Four!' and uproar.*

(*A wicket-keeper can be used.*)

Scene Five

Up right a patch of light falling from a doorway. Above it the dark outline of the bottom part of an inn sign.

SCOPEY *and* PAT *on the floor down left.*

PAT. Where yoo put that thing?

SCOPEY. Thirty beauties.

PAT (*slight burp*). I like Babycham.

SCOPEY *stretches.*

Yoo throw that away?

SCOPEY. What?

PAT. Yoo know.

SCOPEY. Why?

PAT. That ent nice for someone a find.

SCOPEY. Things yoo fret 'bout, gal. Oo'd know it was us?

PAT. 'Ave yoo throwed it?

SCOPEY. Yeh.

PAT. O. (*Pause.*) Yoo're a real devil, ent yoo?

SCOPEY. With one 'orn.

PAT (*laughs shrilly*). Not agen?

SCOPEY. Sh!

PAT (*giggling*). They 'ear?

SCOPEY. Oo cares?

PAT. I ent 'avin' a lot a owd talk.

SCOPEY. Ooo cares?

PAT. Yoo're all right.

SCOPEY. Eh?

PAT. Yoo're a boy.

SCOPEY. Sure?

PAT. Cheeky sod.

SCOPEY. I'll tell yoo somethin', gal – yoo make a fair owd lay.

PAT. That's all yoo want.

SCOPEY. What?

PAT. Yoo know.

SCOPEY. Too shy a say it? Eh?

PAT. Stop pullin' my leg.

SCOPEY. The owd crutch piece – what's wrong with that?

PAT. I'll tell my fiancé.

SCOPEY. Sh!

PAT (*after a pause*). What?

SCOPEY. I thought I 'eard 'em.

PAT. Bill'll be mad when 'e find that's gone.

SCOPEY. 'E's too pissed a notice.

PAT. That boy don't miss much.

SCOPEY. We only 'ad a loan on it.

PAT. Yoo did.

SCOPEY. All right. (*Slight pause.*) Wham! Chriss, that shook 'em!

PAT. You look beautiful all in white.

SCOPEY. That second ball on the last over.

PAT. Sounds like a bride.

SCOPEY. I bet that got the wind up yer, ent it?

PAT. What one was that?

SCOPEY. I knew what I was playin' at, though, boy. I weren't takin' no chances.

PAT. O, don't touch the grass.

SCOPEY. No?

PAT. That's wet.

SCOPEY. Yoo're 'and's wet, ent it?

    RON *comes in up right. He carries a glass.*

RON. Sco? (*Pause.*) They're drinkin' yoor beer, boy! (*Pause.*) Well 'e ent 'ere?

RON *goes off up right, whistling.*

PAT. I thought 'e'd saw us.

SCOPEY. Oo cares?

PAT. I 'ont 'avin' no talk.

SCOPEY. I'll shut 'em up.

PAT. That's what I'm afraid of.

SCOPEY. Sh a minute.

PAT. What?

SCOPEY. Sh.

PAT. Why? (*Pause.*) Well?

SCOPEY. Nice, ent it?

PAT. What is?

SCOPEY. Lyin' 'ere.

PAT. Why?

SCOPEY. Quiet.

PAT. Yoo pullin' my leg?

SCOPEY. Don't yoo like it?

PAT. It's a bit cold, ent it?

SCOPEY. Yoo cold, gal?

    PAT *giggles.*

    BYO *and* RON *come up right. Pause.* BYO *sighs. Pause.*

RON. That's better.

BYO. Shake it more'n ten times an' yoo're playin' with it.

    They laugh.

RON. Yoo're pissed, boy.

BYO. I'm pissed?

RON. That's right.

BYO. I ent.

RON. Yoo're pissed.

BYO. Yoo're pissed. boy.

RON. Can't even slash straight.

BYO. Yoo wait till I finished 'fore yoo say that, yoo owd devil.

RON. Listen. (*He throws a stone. A splash.*) Yoo can't 'it that owd pond.

    c

BYO. No? (*He throws a stone. A splash.*) Aaah! Oo's pissed? (*He throws a stone. A splash.*) Aaah! Fair owd noise, ent it?

RON. Eh?

BYO. Fair owd noise.

RON. Yoo're pissed.

BYO. Listen. (*He throws a stone. A splash.*) Aaah!

RON. Yoo're pissed, boy, doo yoo 'ont never stand out 'ere throwin' stones. (*He tries to push* BYO.) Pissed!

BYO. That's nice out 'ere. I'd like to stay out 'ere all night. Quiet.

RON. Quiet?

BYO. Eh?

RON. With that pissy row?

BYO. That don't count. That's out the back.

RON. My life, boy. Yoo pissed.

BYO. Next door.

RON. Yoo comin'?

BYO. Quiet.

RON. Yoo'll fall in that pond.

BYO. Quiet!

> *In the pub they start to sing 'He's a Jolly Good Fellow'.* RON *joins in.*

RON (*toasting*). All the best! Where's yoor beer?

BYO. Inside.

RON. Yoo ent likely a see that no more.

BYO. I'd better. (*Turns right.*) What thievin' bastard took my beer?

RON (*following him*). 'E's 'ad too much all ready.

> RON *and* BYO *go off up right.*

PAT. Wait till I tell the gals tmorra. Oi, that damp'll be comin' through.

SCOPEY. Howd still a minute.

PAT. Lazy sod.

SCOPEY. I earnt a rest.

PAT (*giggles*). Yoo should a gone in when they was singin'.

SCOPEY. They'll 'ave t' doo without me.

PAT. I'd like a throw stones in that pond. When yoo gooin' in?

SCOPEY. Ent yoo gooin' a try an' keep me 'ere?

PAT. We're missin' all the drink.

SCOPEY. I'll buy yoo all the drink yoo want anytime.

PAT. Oo's money yoo throwin' away?

SCOPEY. When a gal lays like yoo, mate, she can 'ave anythin'.

PAT. Stop it.

SCOPEY. Come on.

PAT. Fancy yoo askin'.

SCOPEY. Ha!

PAT (*after a pause*). Howd me tight. (*Pause.*) Yoo looked beautiful
    this afternoon. (*Slight pause.*) I keep seein' yoo standin' there
    with that bat.

SCOPEY. I felt all right.

PAT. D'yoo like me?

SCOPEY. What yoo think?

PAT. 'Ow many gals yoo been with?

SCOPEY. Enough.

PAT. Yoo can't remember. (*Cross.*) No.

SCOPEY. Come on, yoo like it.

PAT. We ought a goo in.

SCOPEY. Please.

    Pause.

  Fag?

PAT. Now?

SCOPEY. Yeh.

PAT. No.

SCOPEY. First time I 'eard that.

PAT. An' the last.

BILL (*off*). Pat!

PAT. 'E's after 'is sheet.

SCOPEY. Good luck.

PAT. Better put it back.

SCOPEY. Ground's wet.

PAT. 'E'll goo mad.

SCOPEY. Let 'im.

PAT. I told yoo not a take it.

SCOPEY. It's all right.

PAT. Yoo'd better 'ave a good story.

SCOPEY. Sure.

PAT. An' don't bring me into it.

SCOPEY. I won't.

PAT. Well, I 'ont 'avin' no trouble.

SCOPEY. Pat.

VOICE (*off*). Last orders, lads.

PAT. What?

SCOPEY. Let's goo under the trees.

PAT. That's too wet.

SCOPEY. Come on.

VOICE (*off*). Drink up, lads.

PAT. Why?

SCOPEY. It's still early.

PAT. No.

SCOPEY. They're comin' out now.

PAT. Too dark.

SCOPEY. Let me screw yoo agen, Pat. I got to.

PAT. Can we take the sheet?

SCOPEY. Yeh. That'll goo around us, an' over the top.

    PAT *laughs*.

  Howd on a me 'and.

PAT. Yoo ought a goo in once afore it's finished.

SCOPEY. They 'ont see us over there.

PAT. Goo in an' say good night.

SCOPEY. I'd never get out.

PAT. I lost my bag.

SCOPEY. I got it.

PAT. Where's the sheet?

SCOPEY. 'Ere.

PAT. Ooo.

SCOPEY. What's up?

PAT. It's wet.

SCOPEY. Goo steady. That's the pond.

PAT. I'll tell me gran I slept with June.

SCOPEY. I'll find a dry spot we can stay the whole night, gal.

PAT. No.

SCOPEY. Sure.

    PAT *and* SCOPEY *go out up left.*

JOE (*off*). I reckon 'e were dodgin' 'is round.

    LEN *comes up right.*

LEN. Sco should a stayed. That looked bad.

BYO (*off*). I reckon 'e's just wore out.

    BYO *and* JOE *come on after* LEN.

LORRY. I reckon 'e can doo what 'e like.

JOE. Eh?

    LORRY *comes in after the others.*

BILL (*off*). Pat!

LORRY. 's obvious.

JOE. 'Ow?

LORRY. Whatever 'e doo I reckon 'e's great.

JOE. Great?

LORRY. Great!

JOE. My life! That's luck.

BYO. Wrap up, yoo nits.

    BILL *comes in down right.*

BYO. No luck?

BILL. No.

BYO. Should never a left it on that bike in the first place. I told yoo enough.

LORRY. T'ent likely yoo'll see that agen, boy.

BILL. If that's gone, that's gone. Good 'ealth. (*Takes a small bottle of rum from inside his shirt. Drinks.*)

BYO. That's a boy. (*Takes the bottle from* BILL. *Drinks.*) Good owd Billy, then.

LORRY. Yoo'll be sick.

BYO. Over yoo, I 'ope. Taste.

LORRY (*takes the bottle. Drinks*). 'Andsome.

JOE. I'm 'ere.

BYO. We can smell yer.

JOE (*takes bottle. Drinks*). Aaaaaaaaaaaaaaaah!

LORRY. Let's goo round Sco's place.

BYO. No.

BILL. Nit.

LORRY. They reckon 'e's been out trainin' on the common early mornin's for months.

BYO. Rum boy.

RON. 'E must a been countin' on gettin' in the team some time.

LORRY. Chriss 'e knocked owd man Bullright all over the place, ent 'e?

JOE. Let's goo an' turn owd Alen's dump over.

BILL. Doo what?

JOE. Smash 'is windows.

BYO. Yeh.

RON. Dirty owd diddy boy.

BILL. 'E ent got no windows.

BYO. Well, smash 'is 'ead in.

JOE. Yeh.

BILL. Nits.

BYO. Eh?

BILL. Nits. I ent runnin' round that owd drain 'ole in the dark.

BYO. Come on, just for a laugh.

BILL. Up t' yoor eyes in cess. Goo on, goo. (*Shakes the bottle against his ear.*) Goo.

JOE. Yoo never want a doo nothin'. Yoo 'ont got no goo, boy.

BYO. Much left?

BILL. Ent nearly started.

BYO. I'll stay 'ere a see yoo get 'ome, boy, doo yoo'll be sleepin' in the ditch.

BILL. Let's sit be the 'edge an 'ave a natter.

BYO (*to* JOE). Get lost.

Scene Six

ALEN's *place.*

PAT *sweeps the floor. She picks up a paper and puts it on the pile by the door. She goes on sweeping.*

PAT. I 'ont got no goo in me today. That'll 'ave t'o doo with just a lick.

    ALEN *takes the paper from the pile and puts it back on the floor.*
Why don't yoo put the dut back?

ALEN. That'll get back be itself.

PAT. Yoo'll 'ave t' eat on bread and tatters tmorra. Doo yoo good. Give them owd pipes a rest. (*She sweeps round the table.*) I don't reckon all that owd tin stuff doo anyone's insides no good. Yoo need proper meals. Why yoo don't goo out the back an' dig that little patch, yoo'd 'ave a proper little garden for vegetables out there. Tins. I 'ad a doze dinner time. (*She leans the broom against the wall.*) That look better. Doo till tmorra, anyroad. I'll see if I can't get 'ere early. I ent promisin', mind. (*She puts on her coat.*) I never thought I'd like watchin' that owd cricket. I keep seein' 'im chargin' up an' down in 'is white. (*She picks up her bag and goes towards the door.*)

ALEN. List.

PAT. O yes. Where's my pencil. I 'ad that in the back a my mind but I couldn't think what that was. (*She sits at the table, tears a strip from a paper and starts to write.*) One stew. Three beans. Two large rice. One bread. One fancy. Four ounces boiled. Half tea. That's all, ent it? Yoo got plenty a bread and tatters a see yoo through tmorra. (*She looks in the large bin on the table. She adds to the list.*) Half butter. Then you can fill up in the evenin'. Eggs. (*She takes a folded shopping bag from the table drawer and goes to the door.*) Cheerio.

ALEN. Vaporated.

PAT. I knew I left somethin'.

ALEN. One vaporated.

PAT. I'll remember that.

ALEN. Yoo put that down.

PAT *goes back to the table and writes on the list.*

Yoo 'ad no right to leave that off in the first place.

PAT. I got other things to remember.

ALEN. One vap. Don't yoo start comin' 'ere 'alf asleep on yoor feet.

PAT. I 'ont takin' my orders from yoo.

ALEN. One vap. Yoo put that down.

PAT. I got it down. (*She goes back to the door.*)

ALEN. An' don't yoo come 'ere forgettin'.

PAT. I'll come 'ow I like.

ALEN. One vap. My milk.

PAT. I 'ope they sold out.

ALEN. Yoo bring that.

PAT. I'll bring your bloody milk.

ALEN. I need my milk same as – listen!

PAT. What?

ALEN. Oo's outside?

PAT. No one.

ALEN. Someone snoopin'.

PAT. Ow d'yoo know?

ALEN. Listen.

PAT. I can't 'ear nothin'. I expect Bill's come t' meet me.

ALEN. 'E whistles an' kicks the stones. Someone's tryin' t' be quiet.

PAT. Leave off, yoo'll give yoorself the creeps.

ALEN. Don't goo through the door.

PAT. Yoo're daft.

ALEN. Don't.

PAT. Cheerio.

ALEN. 'E's one a yoor men.

PAT. Don't be daft, boy.

ALEN. I towed yoo afore I 'ont 'avin' that sort 'angin' round my door.

PAT. What sort?

ALEN. Roughs.

PAT. I'll be in tmorra. (*She starts to open the door.*)

ALEN. Yoo 'ont peeled my tatties.

PAT. Yoo'll 'ave t' peel 'em.

ALEN. That's yoor place t' peel 'em.

PAT. Once 'ont never cripple yoo.

ALEN. Yoo swore t' yoor mum be 'er dyin' bed yoo'll peel my tatties.

PAT. I did not.

ALEN. Liar.

PAT. All I ever said was I'd see yoo kep clean an' swep out.

ALEN. 'E's creepin' be the side.

PAT. After today yoo peel yoor own tatters or bloody well 'ave 'em in their jackets.

ALEN. Yoo swore by yoor dead mum's body.

PAT. I don't give a damn what I swore then, that's what I'm swearin' now.

ALEN. 'E ent moved. 'E must be out the back.

PAT. Yoo been 'ere too long. I said it'd turn yoor 'ead, boy.

ALEN. Dirty owd diddies scratchin' be me door, no decent vittels, no milk, an' all me own cookin' a cope with an' I 'ont 'ardly got the grip in me 'ands a gimp howd on a knife count a me cripplin'.

PAT. That'll learn yoo not a row.

ALEN. Yoor mum's turnin' in 'er grave.

PAT. For Chriss' sake don't keep on about 'er.

ALEN. I ent long for this world. I can't draw me breath today.

PAT. That's a lot a owd tommy rot. All yoo need's a dose a fresh air an' a good scrubbin'.

ALEN. Then why yoo swep all that dut flyin' up?

PAT. Yoo should a let me open that door.

ALEN. All me mates is gone.

PAT. Yoo're sure I got all the shoppin' down.

ALEN. T'ent no use, yoo'll forget 'alf on it, anyroad.

PAT. Then I'm off. I'm late.

ALEN. One a these days yoo'll get tired a comin', I can see it. I'll die a starvin' or be killed up on the road tryin' a reach the 'ouses.

PAT. Ta-ta.

ALEN. I can throw out my messages in them little bottles agen, gal. Yoo howd yoor tongue doo I –

PAT. No yoo don't, my boy. I 'ont 'avin' that agen. Yoo come the owd acid with me an' yoo goo straight back on yoor rations: salt beef an' one 'alf cup a water per day.

ALEN. No.

PAT. I'll turn off the mains on the road an' I don't see yoo gooin' down there t' turn it back.

ALEN. Wicked!

PAT. Yoo count your blessin's an' close yoor mouth.

ALEN. Turnin' in 'er grave.

PAT. I 'ope the exercise doo 'er good.

> PAT *goes out through the door* – ALEN *gestures to stop her and groans. He bolts the door and turns the key. He bends down and puts his ear to the door. He straightens and tilts his head back a little, still with his ear to the door. Pause. He turns uncertainly back to the room. He turns back to the door and listens. Suddenly he scurries down left and stands behind the table. He is shaken with convulsions. His throat rattles. He panics. Pause. He gains a little control.*

SCOPEY (*off*). Pat.

> ALEN *starts to shake again. He tries to muffle the rattle in his throat.*

SCOPEY (*off*). Pat there?

> ALEN *scurries up to the bed and crouches behind it with his back to the wall. He starts to pull the bed towards him. It squeaks. He stops.*

SCOPEY (*off*). Oi!

> ALEN *pulls the bed again. It squeaks. He stops.*

SCOPEY (*off*). Yoo can 'ear. (*Pause.*) What yoo doo all day? *Longer pause.*

> ALEN *rises from behind the bed and strains towards the wall.*

What yoor 'obbies?

ALEN *ducks behind the bed again. Pause.*

Pat? (*Pause.*) She must a gone. (*Pause. Farther away*) – Sorry, mate.

Silence.

Scene Seven

The open.
A bench down left.
JUNE *and* PAT *sit on the bench. They eat sandwiches.*

PAT. Nice?

JUNE. No.

PAT. Chriss.

JUNE. I'll 'ave t' try gettin' up early an dooin' me own.

PAT. Yoo ought a ask 'er t' get somethin' nice in. Tell 'er. They 'ont use no imagination.

JUNE. I say anythin' an' she say what yoo expect for three pound.

PAT. Got a fag?

JUNE. No.

PAT. Yoo ent looked.

JUNE. I know I 'ont got none. I smoke my last tea break.

PAT. I left four in the clock. Gran'll swipe them.

JUNE. Yoo'll 'ave t' goo without.

PAT. Sco'll 'ave some.

JUNE (*opening a magazine*). If 'e get 'ere.

PAT. Yoo should a brought the cards.

JUNE. Yoo owe me three an' two.

PAT. Chriss.

JUNE (*going through the magazine*). Yoo told 'im anything.

PAT. What about?

JUNE. Ent yoo 'ad a talk?

PAT. What for?

JUNE. 'Bout Bill and them.

PAT. No.

JUNE. O. (*Pause.*) Ent 'e said?

PAT. What about?

JUNE. Fellas?

PAT. No.

JUNE. Didn't 'e notice?

PAT. 'E was too pissed a notice.

JUNE. Some people 'ave all the luck.

PAT. I just said 'ow' and 'e said it won't 'urt next time, you'll see.

JUNE. Saucy sod.

PAT. Then 'e wanted a take a chance.

JUNE. Yoo said no.

PAT. I said if yoo don't treat me with respect yoo ent 'avin' it.

JUNE. Yes.

PAT. I could doo with a fag.

JUNE (*reopening the magazine*). I still think yoo should a told 'im.

PAT. That ent nothin' a doo with 'im.

JUNE. Yoo're supposed a start off tellin' everythin' like that.

PAT. 'E can look after 'is business an' I'll look after mine.

JUNE. Yoo're scared, gal.

PAT. What for?

JUNE. It might put 'im off.

PAT. Don't be bloody daft.

JUNE. Fellas can be funny.

PAT. They know when they're on to a good thing.

JUNE. Yoo bein' married in white?

PAT. No money.

JUNE. Where yoo gooin' away?

PAT. If we get howd on a place we'll 'ave the decoratin' a doo. I'd rather see that done first an' goo away for a good week next year.

JUNE. Did I tell yoo that joke?

PAT. No.

JUNE. 'Bout the honeymoon couple.

PAT. No.

JUNE. It's a laugh.

PAT. Well goo on.

JUNE. Well they goo a this 'otel, see, an' they goo upstairs an' the bloke 'e say I'm just gooin' downstairs for a packet a fags, dear.

PAT. I could doo with a fag.

JUNE. Listen. So 'e goo downstairs an' she get undressed an' 'ops into bed on account a bein' shy, see, an' suddenly there's this big bangin' on the door.

PAT. Yes.

JUNE. A big bangin'. An' she shout out 'No need a knock, dear. I ent afraid' an' 'e say 'Yoo would be if yoo knew what I was knockin' on the door with.'

PAT. That's good, ent it.

JUNE. Bang bang.

PAT. Bang bang. 'Oo told yoo that?

JUNE. My mum.

PAT. She know some lovely stories, don't she.

JUNE. There 'e is.

PAT (*waves*). Oi.

JUNE. Suppose Bill or one a 'em say somethin'?

PAT. 'E's been knockin' about with that crowd long afore I went with 'im. If 'e want a know, 'e know by now. (*Calls.*) Fags?

    SCOPEY *comes in from the right.*   .

SCOPEY. I only got a roll.

JUNE. Take the weight off yoor feet.

SCOPEY (*sitting*). An' on t' me arse.

PAT. If it ent corns it's piles.

JUNE. Like a sandwich?

SCOPEY. No.

PAT. Goo on.

SCOPEY. I 'ad mine.

PAT. Busy?

SCOPEY. Usual.

JUNE. Terrible this mornin'.

SCOPEY. Shall I doo yoo a roll?

PAT. I'll doo it.

> SCOPEY *hands her the pouch, papers and roller. She rolls a*
> *cigarette.*

SCOPEY. Goo steady with that bacco. That's got a last.

JUNE. Can she roll one for me?

SCOPEY. Sure.

PAT. Trust yoo.

SCOPEY. No, that's all right.

PAT. I 'ad a postcard from Betty Legs.

SCOPEY. O.

PAT. They reckon 'er 'usband's gooin' a be posted over 'ere agen,
so she'll be comin' across with 'im. (*She opens her bag.*)

JUNE. Doo she say when?

PAT. No.

> PAT *hands the card to* SCOPEY. *He looks at it and at the same*
> *time* JUNE *tries to look at it.*

JUNE. Let's see.

SCOPEY. Don't snatch – What's that?

PAT. Nice, ent it?

SCOPEY. What is it?

PAT. That's where she lives. They call it a city but that ent no
bigger than a little town.

JUNE. Nice.

SCOPEY. Yoo can't tell.

JUNE. I like it.

SCOPEY. Yoo need more than that. Yoo'd 'ave t' see more.

JUNE. It's nice.

SCOPEY. Yoo need more.

JUNE. I know what I like – they keep the streets swep.

SCOPEY. Where yoo seen streets like that?

JUNE. Only count a people drop dirt all the time. People are pigs.

SCOPEY. Nothin's like that. No more yoo ent seen sky like that.

JUNE. Never said I 'ad. I just said I like it.

SCOPEY. Yoo can't tell. Where's the people an' the corners? (*He*
turns the card over.)

PAT. Thanks.

SCOPEY (*reads*). 'Ope yoo are keepin' well an yoor family. We are are well but baby does not like the heat. Hyram say 'e may be posted 'ome, 'e 'ear rumour. So look forward to seen' yoo soon. Love to all, Betty, Baby, Hyram. That don't say a word what's on the front.

JUNE. She ent got that much room, 'ave she.

PAT. Let's 'ave it. (*She puts the card back in her bag.*)

SCOPEY (*sniffs*). I'd like a stick postcards all over the room.

PAT. Give me a light.

    JUNE *hands her matches. She lights her cigarette.*

SCOPEY. On the floor an' the ceilin'.

PAT. Talk about somethin' else.

JUNE. Cheap wall paper.

PAT. We'll 'ave t' get a wall first.

JUNE. I know what 'e's after. Dirty owd man.

SCOPEY. What?

PAT. Arse an' tit.

SCOPEY. I never said that.

JUNE. Well what?

SCOPEY. Just pictures.

PAT. Why?

SCOPEY. Why? That's what I'd like.

PAT. Not in my place.

JUNE. Yoo said she could doo me a roll.

SCOPEY. Sure.

PAT. Can I borrow it?

SCOPEY. All right.

PAT. Yoo can 'ave it back tonight.

SCOPEY. Okay.

JUNE. Ta.

Scene Eight

ALEN's.

ALEN *alone. He stands at the table. He is opening a tin. He puts the tin opener in his overcoat pocket. He drinks the juice from the tin. He starts to put the tin back on the table. A knock. He snatches his hand away from the tin and half turns right – there are no other reactions. Pause. A knock – not as loud as the first.*

SCOPEY (*off*). Oi. (*A knock.*) She left 'er bag. (*Pause.*) Yoo got 'er bag.

ALEN. She's gone.

SCOPEY. Open this. (*He bangs on the door.*)

ALEN. Yoo'll catch 'er up.

SCOPEY. She'll want that bag when she find she ent got it.

ALEN. She's gone.

SCOPEY (*banging on door*). I'll kick it open.

ALEN. Howd on. (*He goes right, trying to think.*)

SCOPEY. Well?

ALEN. No shoppin' tmorra –

SCOPEY. I want that bag.

ALEN. – that's Tuesday.

SCOPEY. I know yoo got it.

ALEN. That's Tuesday.

SCOPEY. I warned yoo.

ALEN (*angrily*). No!

SCOPEY (*after a pause*). What yoo dooin' now? (*Slight pause.*) I bet yoo get up t' some fancy tricks, boy. In there be yoorself all day (*Pause.*) I could easy get my mates up 'ere. Easy.

ALEN. The police 'ont –

SCOPEY. Police! That's a laugh. They're just waitin' for a chance a get yoo out, boy. They don't reckon yoor sort anywhere. They just moved the gypsies on. I could stop Pat comin 'ere. Anytime.

ALEN (*after a pause*). Wait up on the road. I'll throw it out.

SCOPEY. Open this door!

ALEN. Yoo can't stop 'er comin'.

SCOPEY. What yoo want 'er for? (*Slight pause.*) What yoo two get
up to?

ALEN. I'm ill.

SCOPEY. What?

ALEN (*goes to the bed. Slight pause.* SCOPEY *kicks the door violently*).
Don't kick my door! I'm ill! I'm ill!

SCOPEY (*kicks the door*). I'm comin', mister!

ALEN. Stop it! (*He goes to the door and opens it.*)

SCOPEY. 'Urry up.

> The door is opened. SCOPEY *steps in. Pause.*

Smoke?

ALEN. Eh.

SCOPEY. Smoke? Fag? Roll? Cheroot, mister.

ALEN. Eh.

SCOPEY. Shame. I'm out. (*He looks at the oil cookers.*) She lug that
oil all the way up in winter. She's a strong gal, ent she? (*Pause.*)
Yoo collect papers.

> ALEN *holds out a purple and brown leatherette bag.*

Stinks. Can't yoo smell it? Coo.

ALEN. Yoo goo.

SCOPEY. Eh?

ALEN. Yoo don't like it. (*He holds out the bag.*)

SCOPEY. I bet the council ent been round 'ere. What's on the
turn?

ALEN. I like it.

SCOPEY. This?

ALEN. Eh?

SCOPEY. Puttin' it down?

ALEN. Eh?

SCOPEY. Grub? (*He taps the opened tin of pears.*)

ALEN. No, no.

SCOPEY. Guts.

ALEN. Bag.

D

SCOPEY. I ent invited?

ALEN. Eh?

SCOPEY. Yoo don't believe in sharin'.

ALEN. Nothin'. Not eatin'.

SCOPEY. Yoo ought a wash yoor 'ands afore yoo get up t' table. (*He goes up to the stack of papers by the wall, picks up a sheaf, glances at them, and whacks them down on the couch.*) What they for?

ALEN. My bloody work!

SCOPEY. What?

ALEN. Yoo cow!

SCOPEY. Do what?

    ALEN's *anger cools and he is afraid.*

Eh? Yoo cow? What's up? (*Pause.*) What work? (*He goes to* ALEN.) Why d'yoo blow yoor top? (*Pause.*)

ALEN. Bag.

SCOPEY. What's the paper for? That yoor work? (*Pause.*) Ha!

    ALEN *sits on the bed.*

What's this for? (*Touches a box with his boot.*) What's this? (*He taps the couch with his boot. Pause.*) Yoo ought a keep a dog. Good company. She 'ont kep yoo all that clean. Oi, I'm marryin' 'er. She said? (*Pause. He takes the bag from the bed.*) Didn't recognize it. Looks different out there. (*Pause. Sniffs.*) Coo. (*Slight pause.*) Can yoo lock up all right?

ALEN. Lock?

SCOPEY. She told me yoo was a grippin' owd bastard. I'll leave the bag, I forgot that was Tuesday amorra. Oi, yoo tellin' 'er I been 'ere?

ALEN. What?

SCOPEY. Don't. Don't. All right? Doo it'll get back a me an' I'll want a know why, mate. I 'ont never been out 'ere an' yoo 'ont seen nothin' of me. (*He stands at the door.*) I'll shut it behind me.

    SCOPEY *goes out through the door.* ALEN *goes halfway towards the door. He stops. He stoops slightly and stretches his neck with the concentration of listening.*

(*Off.*) 'Night.
> *Pause.* ALEN *goes quietly to the door. He locks it.*

Scene Nine

SCOPEY'*s and* PAT'*s place.*
A table left. A portable bed up right. At the moment it has been put out of the way up right, where it lies against the wall. Two chairs.
PAT *and* SCOPEY. *They talk in the clichés of argument, but they sound friendly.*
Dark.

PAT. Yoo should a kep it by the fuse box.

SCOPEY. That's a fat lot a help.

PAT. Then yoo wouldn't be lookin' for it.

SCOPEY. Why don't yoo keep it by the fuse box?

PAT. That ent my place.

> *Pause.* SCOPEY *looks in the needlework box.*

That ent there. Goo an' borrow next door.

SCOPEY. Where's our'n?

PAT. Yoo won't find that in a month a Sundays.

SCOPEY. It can't walk.

PAT. Perhaps we used it.

SCOPEY. When?

PAT. Don't ask me.

SCOPEY. Well when? We 'ont 'ad no call a use it. If that's gone, that little Joany twist it up for 'er brooches every time yoo 'ave 'er up 'ere.

PAT. She ent been 'ere often. Yoo can't blame 'er.

SCOPEY. That's where that's gone.

PAT. More like yoo lost it.

SCOPEY. Sure. (*He sits at the table.*)

PAT. Yoo can't see t' finish yoor dinner.

SCOPEY. I know where the 'ole is.

PAT. Ent yoo mendin' that fuse then?

SCOPEY. That'll wait. I'm 'ungry, gal.

PAT. Yoo ent better make a mess a my clean cloth.

SCOPEY. I 'ont make no mess.

PAT (*after a pause*). Finish off that ice cream?

SCOPEY. Yep.

PAT. Nice, ent it.

SCOPEY. Yep.

PAT. That 'ont keep, anyhow. I 'ad another card from Betty.

SCOPEY. Yeh?

PAT. She ent comin'.

SCOPEY. No?

PAT. They posted 'im t' Germany.

SCOPEY. O.

PAT. I suppose she'll be comin' over t' visit.

SCOPEY. They got the money. What's the picture?

PAT. I'll show yoo when we got some light.

SCOPEY. Say anythin'?

PAT. Not much.

SCOPEY (*after a pause*). What she say?

PAT. She ent comin'. (*Pause.*) I can't see t' put the kettle on.

SCOPEY. Open a bottle.

PAT. I ent scaldin' myself t' death just 'cause yoo're too bloody lazy a mend a fuse.

SCOPEY. I can't find the wire.

PAT. Yoo ent looked.

SCOPEY (*after a pause*). I'll get the bed out.

PAT. Yoo can't goo a bed fore yoo fixed that fuse.

SCOPEY. 'Course I can.

PAT. Yoo ent done the washin' up.

SCOPEY. That'll be there in the mornin'. Then I can see what I'm dooin'.

PAT. Suppose there's an emergency.

SCOPEY. There won't be.

PAT. Suppose the 'ouse catch fire?

SCOPEY. Then there'll be plenty a light. (*Eats.*) All the wirin's US in this place.

PAT. That ent this place. That's just that owd fuse blowed.

SCOPEY. They ought a knocked this owd 'eap down afore the war. The first one.

PAT. Yoo shouldn't a lost the wire.

SCOPEY. What?

PAT. Soon's we get enough t' lay down we'll start lookin' round.

SCOPEY. When's that?

PAT. Yoo ought a brighten this place up.

SCOPEY. Why? I 'ont got no interest. I 'ont wastin' my time on somethin' belongs some other bloke.

PAT. Yoo're usin' it.

SCOPEY. I'm payin' for it.

PAT. Pass yoor plate.

SCOPEY (*passes his plate*). I could meet yoo out a work tmorra an' we could goo see that new estate be Dunmow.

PAT. What's the use on it? We 'ont got no deposit.

SCOPEY. It'll give us some ideas.

PAT. Yoo got plenty a them. That's Thursday tmorra – I doo owd Alen's.

SCOPEY. So.

PAT. Be the time I'm clear a that that'll be too late.

SCOPEY. That owd sod gets on my wick.

PAT. That 'ont 'is fault I 'ave t' goo there.

SCOPEY (*annoyed*). 'Oo's is it then? Yoo spend more time up there than yoo doo in my 'ome.

PAT (*annoyed*). Don't be a liar.

SCOPEY (*annoyed*). I 'ont 'avin' yoo galavantin' up there soon's ever I turn my back.

PAT. I don't like gooin'.

SCOPEY. Suppose we moved out.

PAT. How?

SCOPEY. Suppose we moved out.

PAT. Well we ent.

SCOPEY. We will one day.

PAT. Then we'll 'ave t' see.

SCOPEY. I reckon I pass 'is owd sty every time I come 'ome a work. I can easy keep an eye on 'im.

PAT. That ent a case a keep an eye. Yoo 'ave t' keep him swep' an' clean an' that.

SCOPEY. There's nothin' a that – just poke the owd broom round the corners.

PAT. I'll remember that next time I ask yoo t' doo somethin'. 'Oo doo 'is bits a shoppin'?

SCOPEY. Yoo doo that an' I'll drop it in when I goo.

PAT. 'E'd never let yoo in.

SCOPEY. 'E's too fond a 'is owd gut t' starve.

PAT. Yoo ent serious?

SCOPEY. Sure, if it helps.

PAT. Well . . . I ent thought about it. I always gone up there. I'd feel queer without. Chriss knows I've 'ad my share a slavin' for 'im.

SCOPEY. An' all for nothin'.

PAT. Not so much as a thankyoo. Yoo could try it for a bit an' see 'ow that work. That ent no 'arm.

SCOPEY. If it don't work yoo'll just 'ave a goo back.

PAT. Yes.

SCOPEY. Give us a 'and with the bed.

PAT. O yoo're nice when yoo want a be!

SCOPEY. Come on. It was late agen last night. That 'ont give yoo no time.

PAT. Didn't stop yoo.

SCOPEY. That was just arsin' about. What kep yoo, anyway?

PAT. Nosey bugger.

SCOPEY. I'll find out. (*He lifts the bed from the wall.*)

PAT. I ent gooin' a bed yet. That's too early.

SCOPEY. Get the pillows an' shut up.

PAT. Yoo tired?

SCOPEY. No.

PAT. Yoo been over-dooin' it, boy.

SCOPEY. Oo say?

PAT. Sheila at work only doo it twice a week.

SCOPEY. 'Er owd man must be knockin' a bit outside.

PAT. Yoo reckon so?

SCOPEY. Stands to reason.

PAT. She ought a try 'elpin' 'erself, then she'd find out.

 SCOPEY *tests the bed with his hand.*

 That's all yoo married me for.

SCOPEY (*making the bed*). It wasn't yoor money.

PAT (*making the bed*). Sorry?

SCOPEY. Not yet.

PAT. Keepin' off the other gals?

SCOPEY. Where was yoo last night?

PAT. Yoo ought a take up a hobby.

SCOPEY. I got one. Tuck it in straight, gal.

 PAT *goes out right.* SCOPEY *gets into bed.* PAT *comes in cleaning*
 her teeth.

PAT. Yoo meant it 'bout the owd boy?

SCOPEY. I said so.

PAT. Did yoo get that glass a beer?

SCOPEY. No pour it out, gal.

 She pours out a glass of beer.

 Get your finger out.

 She hands him the glass.

 Ta.

 PAT *goes out right. Sound of a basin. Sound of running water.*
 She comes back and starts to undress. SCOPEY *gets out of bed.*

PAT. Where yoo gooin'?

SCOPEY. I forgot t' slash. (*He stands the glass down beside the bed.*)
Don't tread in that. (*Goes out right.*)

PAT. I need some new nylons. These a gone 'ome. (*She gets into
bed.*)

Scene Ten

ALEN's *place.*

ALEN *stands alone in the middle of the room.*

A long pause.

SCOPEY (*off*). Yoo can't howd out much longer, doo yoo'll die. (*Pause.*) Can't yoo get it in yoor thick 'ead: she ent comin' no more. (*Pause.*) Yoo want me t' fetch the police? They'll put yoo in the institution straight away. (*Pause.*) I got stew-steak, chips, peas, rice, tea. (*Pause.*) Look 'ere, yoo let me an' when Pat's up an' about she'll take over like she was before. I'll ask 'er anyroad. That's my word. (*Pause.*) Yoo gooin' a die, then?

ALEN. Fetch that gal.

SCOPEY. For Chriss sake – she's ill!

ALEN. Yoo come with 'er.

SCOPEY. She's ill! An' yoo're lettin' me in on my own rights, not me an' 'er! (*Pause.*) If yoo think yoo'll leave it t' the last chance yoo know what'll 'appen. Yoo'll pass out and yoo'll goo afore yoo come round agen. Die in yoor sleep. Yoo sound groggy all ready a me.

> ALEN *opens the door.* SCOPEY *comes in.* ALEN *chokes.*

Yoo're in a fine mess. Sit down. Goo on. I 'ont gooin' a eat yoo.

> ALEN *stands.*

My wife's sorry she can't come, but the doctor 'ont let 'er out a the 'ouse. An' I'll tell yoo somethin' else, soon's she starts 'avin' babies she 'ont be at yoor beck an' call no more. Yoo can't 'ave everythin', boy.

ALEN. Grub.

SCOPEY. All right. She told me 'ow t' doo. Where's yoor tin opener?

> ALEN *takes the opener from his pocket and puts it on the table.*
> SCOPEY *opens a tin of stewed steak.*

She said yoo weren't a good mixer. Yoo 'ad a lot a rows with 'er,

ent yoo. Eh? I ent much of a dab at cookin' but I don't reckon
yoo're used t' the best. If I 'ad any sense I'd just give yoo a cup
a milk an' make yoo wait till tmorra for the rest.

ALEN. No.

SCOPEY. All right, all right. (*He empties tins into pots. He lifts an
empty pot, turns it upside down and bangs the bottom.*) Grubby,
ent it? Don't reckon yoo'll mind, eh? I'm fussy for bein' clean
myself. What yoo two 'ave t' row on? (*He stands the pots on the
cookers.*) Chriss, yoo got 'ords a little vermin runnin' round 'ere.
(*He swipes at the top with a paper.*) Like Ben bloody Hur. (*Slight
pause. He twists the paper and throws it on the ground.*) They'll
shift when it gets 'ot. (*He lights the wicks.*) Yep. (*He slams the
tops down.*) Put the 'eat up their arse. Where yoo keep the
spoons? (*He goes to the table and takes spoons from the drawer. He
goes back to the pots and stirs the food.*) Get yoo up t' the table,
that 'ont be long. Goo on. Bet yoo'd eat anything now, eh? Yoo
never sent Pat yoor best wishes. Eh? Yoo should a said yoo 'ope
she'd be all right. She ent a bad gal, is she. (*He stirs.*) Likes yoo.

ALEN. Ta.

SCOPEY. Eh?

ALEN. Don't like it 'ot, thank 'e.

SCOPEY. Yoo'll 'ave t' 'ave it a bit 'ot, doo yoor stomack 'ont never
howd it.

ALEN. Don't like it 'ot.

SCOPEY. I told 'er yoo was askin' after 'er, else she'd a been upset.
Yoo don't look well. (*Pause.*) Daft sod, yoo should a 'ad me in
first day. All right a wipe up on this? (*He picks up a cloth from
the side of the burners.*)

ALEN. Eh?

SCOPEY. Can I wipe up on this? Them. (*He shows the spoon.*)

ALEN. Me?

SCOPEY. What d'yoo use?

ALEN. Eh?

SCOPEY (*after a pause*). Smells smashin', don't it?

ALEN. That's done now.

SCOPEY. Nearly.

ALEN. Don't like it 'ot.

SCOPEY (*after a pause*). Yoo ought a 'ave radio 'ere.

> *Silence.*

Want me a buy yoo a radio?

> *Silence.*

Yoo can pick 'em up cheap, good second 'and.

> *Silence.*

Sod! I burnt my finger, ent I.

ALEN. That'll doo me.

SCOPEY (*sucks finger*). Get up t' the table. Comin' over. That's
ready now.

> ALEN *sits.*

I'll get a blister there, eh. (*Takes plate from under burner. He
looks at it. He wipes it on the cloth.*) Better. (*He puts the plate in
front of* ALEN *and empties peas on to it.*)

> ALEN *eats.*

Guts! Wait. (*He quickly fetches the steak from the cooker.*) Howd
on! (*He pulls the plate from* ALEN.)

ALEN. Give that 'ere!

SCOPEY. Wait.

ALEN. My plate.

SCOPEY. Yoo'll be sick, gooin' like that. (*He empties the steak on to
the plate. He goes back to the cooker and takes the plate with him.*)

> ALEN *stands.*

I 'ont 'avin' yoo 'oggin that down like that. (*He takes the plate
back to the table.*) Take yoor time, doo yoo'll be sick. (*He puts
the plate in front of* ALEN.) Smells all right. (*Holds* ALEN's *hand
back.*) Now yoo chew on that steady. Chew on it.

> ALEN *lifts his knife and fork. He stops.*

Amen.

> *Pause.* ALEN *pulls the plate a few inches towards him. Pause.*

Why'd I want t' kill yoo, eh?

ALEN. 'Ot.

SCOPEY. Let it stand. Blow on it.

Slight pause. ALEN *grunts.*

If that tastes as good as it smells yoo'll be all right. I reckon I could down that myself.

ALEN *starts to eat, slowly at first.*

Them tins are proper 'andy, ent they. All right? Doo it taste all right mate? Goo steady, then. Whoa! Yoo'll be sick if yoo goo at it like that. (*He pulls the plate away.*)

ALEN. Letsaveit!

SCOPEY. Yoo'll blow yoor stomack up.

ALEN. Giveusere. (*He tries to grab the plate.*)

SCOPEY. Stop it!

ALEN. My plate!

SCOPEY. No! Piggin' like that! (SCOPEY *scoops up a spoonful of food. He holds it in front of* ALEN's *face.*)

ALEN *opens his mouth.*

Wider! (SCOPEY *puts the food into* ALEN's *mouth.*)

ALEN *eats.*

Chew. Goo on, give it a real good chew. No, chew it! (*He holds out the second spoonful.*) Yoo ent 'avin' no more after this if yoo can't chew it properly. (*He puts the food into* ALEN's *mouth.*)

ALEN *eats.*

More than that. Gobblin' like some owd turkey. Pat said yoo're greedy. (*He goes on feeding him.*) Better. What yoo been dooin' since last Thursday? Eh? Chew it. Yoo been washin' yoorself?

ALEN. Howd it straight, boy! Howd on t' it!

SCOPEY. I'll 'ave t' 'ave that coat off an 'ave a good look after. Chew it, goo on. (*He wipes* ALEN's *chin with the cloth.*) No wonder Pat did yoor washin' 'ere. I can't see 'er 'angin' that out our place.

ALEN. What?

SCOPEY. Yoo'll 'ave t' 'elp with yoor own washin' after this.

ALEN. That's good gravy! Don't waste that. That doo yoo a power a good.

SCOPEY. Yoo manage now. (*He gives* ALEN *the spoon.*)

ALEN *scoops up the gravy.* SCOPEY *rights a toppled box.*

I'd better put a broom round 'ere, doo she'll blow my 'ead off.
Where d'yoo keep it?

ALEN. Eh?

SCOPEY. The broom.

ALEN *nods to the wall.*

I should a wore me owd clothes. These're new, like 'em? (*He
tugs at his trouser creases.*) Yoo got an apron, ave yoo?

ALEN. No.

SCOPEY. Patsy must a used one. Where she kep it? (*He takes an
old floral apron from the couch and puts it on.*)

ALEN. Don't want sweepin'.

SCOPEY (*he pushes the broom along the floor*). No? What's that
then? That floor ent been swep since last Christmas. (*Sweeps.
Pause.*) The lads 'd laugh if they saw me. Jazzy, eh? Ent it?
(*Spreads apron.*) I'll 'ave t' come round early tmorra an' give yoo
a good dooin'.

ALEN. What?

SCOPEY. I look a piece, don't I?

ALEN. Yoo comin' tmorra?

SCOPEY. No bother.

ALEN. Send the gal.

SCOPEY. Want a goo 'ungry?

ALEN. When she comin'?

SCOPEY. When she can. (*Sweeps.*) What yoo get up to all day?
Yoo must 'ave plenty a time, yoo ent put a finger t' this place for
months. No more ent she, be the looks on it.

ALEN. Can't sleep with the dut blowin'.

SCOPEY. Eh?

ALEN. Too late for sweepin'.

SCOPEY. Where yoo sleep? That it? (*He looks at the couch.*) Looks
snug enough. Be all right curled up. That's a bit grubby, though,
ent it? (*He sweeps the dirt into a pile by the door.*) Where yoo put
it?

ALEN. Eh?

SCOPEY. I'll chuck it out when I goo. (*Slight pause. He takes off the apron*.) Least that got the worst off. (*He sweeps the dirt into a paper bag, and opens the door a little.* ALEN *grunts and nods to show thanks*.) I thought yoo was gooin' a bed.

ALEN. Eh?

SCOPEY. Ent yoo tired?

ALEN. I goo abed early.

SCOPEY. Don't let me stop yoo.

ALEN. Lock up after yoo.

SCOPEY. I thought yoo might fancy a smoke or a chat. (*Slight pause*.) Yoo don't smoke.

ALEN. Eh?

SCOPEY. Yoo don't smoke.

ALEN. Smoke?

SCOPEY. 'Ow long yoo been 'ere?

ALEN. Don't want no trouble.

SCOPEY. I only asked. Must be fifty years an more since yoo come 'ere. My mum weren't born when yoo come 'ere. (*Pause. He hangs the apron on the wall*.) Ta. That look better 'angin' on a nail. Nice 'ere in a way, ent it. No worry. No one t' nag. My wife'll be wonderin' what I been up to. Yoo ent ever married, 'ave yoo. 'Ow'd yoo doo for sex? (*Pause*.) They say yoo run after Pat's mum one time. But even Pat don't know the truth a that. I bet yoo're a crafty owd sod. Shall I put the kettle on?

ALEN. No.

SCOPEY. I wouldn't put it past yoo t' be 'er dad. I could doo with a cup myself but I reckon there'll be one on my place. We could be in the same family. Bed. Yep. Yoo want your bed an' I could doo with mine. Yoo take a 'ot water bottle?

ALEN. No, no.

SCOPEY. I was gooin' a put the kettle on. I'll get rid a these owd tins for yer. Ha, you could be my dad-in-law. (*He puts the tins in the paper bag*.) I reckon I ent done too bad for a starter. I'll learn. (*Pause*.) I'm off. Don't forget a lock up. (*Pause*.) What's yoor first name?

ALEN. Eh?

SCOPEY. I'm Sco.

ALEN. What?

SCOPEY. That's just a name. (*Shrugs slightly, he goes to the door with the paper bag.*) Anythin' special yoo want brought in?

ALEN. No – I –

SCOPEY. Don't worry, I'll see t' the regular order. (*At door.*) See you, then. (*He goes out. Pause. He pokes his head and half his body back into the room.*) Night.

> SCOPEY *goes out. Pause.* ALEN *goes into the room and listens. He has the plate in his hand. Pause. He bolts the door. He goes to the heap of paper by the wall. He climbs on to it. He spies through a hole in the wall. He steps down. He takes the apron from the nail and puts it back on the bed. He goes to the table. He looks at the empty plate. He picks up the spoon and makes a vague scooping gesture against the plate.*

Scene Eleven

PAT *and* SCOPEY's *place.*

PAT *sits down left at the table.*

SCOPEY *is up right.*

PAT. Yoo workin' late agen t'morra?

SCOPEY. Why?

PAT. If yoo're workin' late I'm gooin' round June's.

SCOPEY. Don't know. Why yoo gooin' round 'er's for?

PAT. Borrow 'er sewin' machine. Can I 'ave a cigarette?

SCOPEY. No.

PAT. Yoo got some.

SCOPEY. Two.

PAT. One each.

SCOPEY. One for me when I goo abed an' one for me when I get up.

PAT. I'm dyin' for a smoke.

SCOPEY. Yoo're always cadgin'.

PAT. Yoo left your rice dinner time.

SCOPEY. So what.

PAT. Weren't that nice, then?

SCOPEY. All right.

PAT. I ent wastin' it. That's got good milk in it. Yoo can 'ave that
cold amorra night. (*Turns a page of the evening paper.*) What time
yoo comin' 'ome?

SCOPEY. When?

PAT. T'morra night.

SCOPEY. Why?

PAT. Don't yoo want your dinner?

SCOPEY. Leave somethin' under the plate.

PAT. That 'ont gooin' a doo yoo no good.

SCOPEY. That'll doo me.

PAT (*after a pause*). I'll 'ave t' take some blue thread round June's.
T'ent likely she'll 'ave that shade. Mais left work t'day. She
comes out so much she look she's 'avin' it t'morra. I feel sorry
for the silly cow. She'll 'ave t' give it away – like the others. She
don't seem t' mind. (*Slight pause.*) I bumped into Bill.

SCOPEY. 'Ow's 'e dooin'?

PAT. Asked about yoo. Said they 'ont seen yoo down the Carpenter's Arms.

SCOPEY. 'Ow's 'e dooin'?

PAT. Fine.

SCOPEY. I ought a look in there some time. I ought a goo amorra
if yoo're gooin' visitin'. I could doo with a night on the beer.

PAT. I told yoo, doo yoo good. (*Turns page.*) We ent been out for
months. (*Turns page.*) Yoo tired agen tonight?

SCOPEY. Eh?

PAT. Yoo tired?

SCOPEY. Why?

PAT. I'm askin'.

SCOPEY. I can't 'elp workin' late. Yoo makin' my cocoa?

PAT. There ent no milk.

SCOPEY. Where's it all gone?

PAT. In the rice puddin'.

SCOPEY. Yoo can't make cocoa without milk.

PAT. That won't 'urt t' 'ave it 'alf an' 'alf for once.

SCOPEY. Yoo know I like it milky. Yoo should a kep' it.

PAT. If yoo keep gettin' this tiredness yoo ought a take somethin'.

SCOPEY. I 'ont gettin' no tiredness. I 'ave t' work 'ard.

PAT. Yoo ought a take some pills t' give yoo a lift.

SCOPEY. Muck.

PAT. What? (*Pause.*) Might make yoo a bit more company 'stead a droopin' all over the place an' droppin' off t' sleep.

SCOPEY. I got a right a be tired when I work late.

PAT. Yoo never used a work late.

SCOPEY. I can't 'elp it if I work late.

PAT. I know.

SCOPEY. I doo all I can for yoo.

PAT. I know.

SCOPEY. What else yoo want?

PAT. I know. Let's goo abed.

> *Silence.*

I'm dyin' for a fag.

> *Silence.*

If yoo're earnin' all that overtime yoo ought a pay me extra. That's only right.

SCOPEY. I'm savin'.

PAT. Where?

SCOPEY. Where?

PAT. Yes.

SCOPEY. That's a daft question.

PAT. Well where?

SCOPEY. I ent tellin' yoo.

PAT. Why?

SCOPEY. That 'ont last long if I tell yoo.

PAT. Other fellas tell their wives.

SCOPEY. They 'ont a married a yoo, mate. Ent yoo puttin' your 'air in curlers t'night?

PAT. I thought yoo'd like me a leave 'em off. Shall I tell Bill yoo'll see 'im?

SCOPEY. When?

PAT. T'morra.

SCOPEY. No.

PAT. Goo out an' get stinkin' drunk, boy. That's what's wrong with yoo.

SCOPEY. No, no. I'll see 'ow it goo.

PAT. If yoo goo yoo'll come in first.

SCOPEY. Why?

PAT. T' change.

SCOPEY. I'll be all right.

PAT. Yoo ent gooin' drinkin' in your owd work clothes.

SCOPEY. Suits me.

PAT. Yoo used a be fussy 'bout your clothes.

SCOPEY. Now what's the matter?

PAT. I ont 'avin' people say I send yoo out any owd 'ow.

SCOPEY. Don't be daft.

PAT. That's 'ow they'll say.

SCOPEY. They can say 'ow they bloody well like, Jack.

PAT. I'm the one 'oo 'as t' listen.

SCOPEY (*Pause. He takes out a cigarette and lights it. He puts the packet back in his jacket pocket, which hangs on the back of a chair*). 'Oo gave owd Alen that watch?

PAT. What watch?

SCOPEY. 'E got an owd watch tucked behind 'is owd coat.

PAT. I never see it.

SCOPEY. What 'e wear under that owd coat?

PAT. Nothin', that wouldn't surprise me.

SCOPEY. Perhaps that clock don't work. That's a rum owd ticker. (*Pause.*) Ent your mum never said why 'e goo shut up like 'e doo?

PAT. I 'ont 'alf a kid when she die. She 'ad me run 'is errands an' say I'd doo 'is cleanin'.

SCOPEY. But why 'e goo like 'e doo in the first place?

PAT. Gone in the 'ead. (*Pause.*) I miss gooin' up there.

E

SCOPEY. Yoo're well out a it.

PAT. That's only 'abit, gooin' up there regular all this time. I never could take to 'im. Dirty owd swine.

SCOPEY. What time is it?

PAT. Gettin' on.

SCOPEY. I thought yoo was gooin' a make my cocoa.

PAT. Yoo said yoo'd goo without.

SCOPEY. I can't sleep on an empty stomach.

PAT. It'll 'ave t' be 'alf an' 'alf.

SCOPEY. I'll 'ave what's left.

PAT. I'm keepin' a drop for the mornin'.

SCOPEY. I can 'ave some a it, anyroad. (*He stands and goes right.*)

PAT. Where yoo gooin'?

SCOPEY. I'll make it.

PAT. Yoo leave some for the mornin', doo I'll start a row.

> SCOPEY *goes out right.* PAT *takes a cigarette from his jacket pocket and lights it. She puts the empty packet back in his pocket.*

SCOPEY (*off*). Yoo nearly run dry on cocoa. T'ent 'ardly 'nough for one cup.

> PAT *starts to smoke. She goes back to the table, sits, and reads the paper.*

SCOPEY (*coming in from the right*). Yoo run out a cocoa. Yoo'll 'ave t' get some in the mornin'.

PAT. I forgot.

SCOPEY. Don't.

PAT (*after a pause*). I pinched one a yoor fags.

SCOPEY. Why?

PAT. I told yoo, I was dyin' for a smoke.

SCOPEY. Yoo want a keep your 'ands off a other people's property.

PAT. That's only an owd smoke.

SCOPEY. That ent the point.

PAT. Mean owd sod.

SCOPEY. I don't mind yoo takin' fags. I towd yoo afore. Yoo take the whole packet if I got 'em. I was savin' that for the mornin'.

PAT. You smoked 'undreds a mine.

SCOPEY. That ent the point.

PAT. Course not!

SCOPEY. That weren't yoor last fag!

PAT. It's only an owd smoke.

SCOPEY. Yoo said that all ready.

PAT. Take 'alf back.

SCOPEY. Thanks!

PAT (*holding out the cigarette*). Well, take the whole bloody lot an'
I'll buy yoo twenty t'morra.

SCOPEY. Don't be bloody saucy.

PAT (*puts the cigarette back in her mouth and draws*). If yoo don't
want it I'll –

    SCOPEY *snatches the cigarette from her mouth. Throws it on the
floor. Stamps and stamps on it.*

SCOPEY. Next bloody time bloody well don't take, ask!

PAT (*shaken*). Thanks. (*She goes up right.*)

SCOPEY. Where yoo gooin'?

PAT. Make myself a cup of tea. I won't use yoor water.

    PAT *goes out right. Pause.* SCOPEY *takes the empty packet from
his jacket pocket. He shakes it. He puts it in his trousers pocket.*

Scene Twelve

ALEN's *place.*

ALEN *lies on the couch.* SCOPEY *sits at the table. He wears the apron.
He is writing the shopping list.*

Pause.

ALEN. Only milk I like come out a tins. (*Pause.*) Count a that's
got the sweet in it already.

SCOPEY (*after a pause*). I'm gooin' a fix this place.

ALEN. What?

SCOPEY. One day I'm gooin' a bring some paint up. A few tins'll
doo this place out nice.

ALEN. Paint only show the dut up.

SCOPEY. Bring the damp out.

ALEN. The smell's bad for the chest.

SCOPEY (*after a pause*). Time yoo been 'ere yoo could a done this place out smashin'.

ALEN. 'Ow owd's yoor dad?

SCOPEY. Eh?

ALEN. What's 'e done? What's 'e got a show?

SCOPEY. I ent got one.

ALEN. Same thing.

SCOPEY (*after a pause*). Yoo ought a burn logs next winter.

ALEN. Logs?

SCOPEY. Save money.

ALEN. I ont 'avin' no owd smelly logs. Can't doo better than para for a good steady 'eat.

SCOPEY. You 'ad ash in that grate afore I shifted it.

ALEN. That's the time I run out a para.

SCOPEY. You can't expect my wife a lug 'eavy owd cans all that way.

ALEN. Yoo said she weren't comin' n' more.

SCOPEY. 'Ow doo yoo know they'll let me goo on dooin' it? (*Pause.*) I was outside last night.

ALEN. I ont 'eard yoo.

SCOPEY. Yoo were asleep.

ALEN. I'd always woke up afore.

SCOPEY. I kep' quiet.

ALEN. Yoo still see owd Mrs Weep's granboys?

SCOPEY. Now'n agen.

ALEN. All that owd crowd?

SCOPEY. Yep.

ALEN. Yoo tell 'em 'bout me?

SCOPEY. No.

ALEN. 'Ave yoo? They know yoo got the key?

SCOPEY. Nope.

ALEN. Yoo ont showed it?

SCOPEY. Yoo don't trust me.

ALEN. I ont never trust Nellie Weep. Shake yoor 'and one minute
an' cut your throat the next.

SCOPEY *folds the shopping bag.*

They 'ere?

SCOPEY. Last night?

ALEN. Yes.

SCOPEY. No.

ALEN. Hm.

SCOPEY. I dug out some owd photographs.

ALEN. Where?

SCOPEY. 'Ere.

ALEN. Yoo been pryin'.

SCOPEY. No.

ALEN. Yoo ont find nothin'.

SCOPEY. 'Oo was she?

ALEN. 'Oo?

SCOPEY. The lady.

ALEN. What lady?

SCOPEY. In the photographs.

ALEN. I ont seen no photographs.

SCOPEY. I found a photograph shaped like an egg, in brown an
white, an' there's fly-blows round the edge.

ALEN. Where is it?

SCOPEY *takes a photograph from his inside jacket pocket. He
sits on the bed with* ALEN. ALEN *looks at the photograph.*

'Oo's she?

SCOPEY. That's what I arst.

ALEN. Ah.

SCOPEY. Well?

ALEN. That's come back. I know 'er. Know 'oo she is?

SCOPEY. No.

ALEN. That come out a that owd scrap shop.

SCOPEY. 'Oo is she.

ALEN. I bought she out a that owd scrap shop stood on the corner
a Dunmow. She were stood out on the pavey in a box. They

knocked that owd shop over years back. She were in three or four a they photographs. They 'ad one a 'er up in a carriage an' 'er dog sat up on the seat aside 'er an a big footman boy stood up the front. 'E was grip howd a the 'orse be the 'ead an' 'e were lookin' straight off that way, but she were starin' straight on yer.

SCOPEY. 'Oo?

ALEN. Fancy that comin' back.

SCOPEY. Yoo kep' the rest?

ALEN. Why'd I buy that owd junk? She could a been dead seventy, eighty year. Perhaps she lie down outside the village.

SCOPEY. Where's the rest?

ALEN. Eh?

SCOPEY. Yoo 'ad some more.

ALEN. Burnt.

SCOPEY. When?

ALEN. Lost. I can't rightly recollect. I used a keep interestin' things. Anythin' interestin'. I'd like a see 'em myself if yoo ferret 'em out.

SCOPEY. What's the shop called.

ALEN. Shop?

SCOPEY. What's the name a the shop, where yoo bought 'em?

ALEN. That's gone.

SCOPEY. In Dunmow.

ALEN. Dunmow.

SCOPEY. What end?

ALEN. Can't think.

SCOPEY. Try.

ALEN. Might a been Saffron.

SCOPEY. Ent you ever seen that lady when yoo was a boy?

ALEN. How?

SCOPEY. Walkin'? Shoppin'? Ridin'?

ALEN. When I were a boy.

SCOPEY (*after a long pause*). Cold now.

ALEN. Years turned.

SCOPEY. I could doo with that primus gooin'.

ALEN. Too early.

SCOPEY. I'll pay.

ALEN. Too early. Once yoo start yoo can't doo without it.

SCOPEY. Yoo're all right in that coat. Let's see you. Take it off.

ALEN. Catch cold.

SCOPEY. Don't yoo take it off a night?

ALEN. Eh?

SCOPEY. I ent never seen yoo outside it.

ALEN. N'more yoo won't.

SCOPEY. Why?

ALEN. Draft round 'ere'll kill yoo. (*He goes to the couch and takes a coat from between the blankets.*)

SCOPEY. Ent killed me.

> ALEN *shows him the coat.*

Looks warm.

ALEN. Like it?

SCOPEY. What's the use. I ont gettin' it.

ALEN. That's good.

SCOPEY. Where d' yoo get it?

ALEN. Dunmow. I bought that same time I bought mine. Market Walden. They make a pair.

SCOPEY. Yoo 'ad it that long?

ALEN. Try it. That's good owd stuff.

SCOPEY (*putting on the coat*). I'd say.

ALEN. Feel that. Thick, ent it.

SCOPEY. Yep.

ALEN. That's an owd army great coat. That goo back long afore the great war.

SCOPEY. She's 'eavy?

ALEN. That keeps the owd draft out.

SCOPEY (*walking up and down*). That's a bit long.

ALEN. That's 'ow yoo want it 'ere.

SCOPEY. That's right. Ta. Doo it make me look bigger, doo it?

ALEN. Yoo can 'ave that.

SCOPEY. I feel bigger.

ALEN. Eh?

SCOPEY. The pockets 'ent 'ere.

ALEN. That's 'ow I bought it.

SCOPEY. No pockets?

ALEN. They're sewed shut.

SCOPEY. 'Oo did that?

ALEN. T' keep the shape.

SCOPEY. Ent yoo 'ad a look?

ALEN. Why?

SCOPEY. There might be somethin' inside.

ALEN. I don't want nothin'.

SCOPEY. Where's the scissors? Yoo get that from that same shop in Dunmow?

ALEN. No scissors 'ere.

SCOPEY. That'll doo. (*He takes a knife from the table.*) Chriss yoo might 'ave anythin' in 'ere. (*He cuts open the tops of the pockets. There is a knock on the door.*)

PAT (*off*). 'Ello!

>SCOPEY *hides himself behind the couch.* ALEN *stares after him. There is another knock.*

'Ello. It's me!

>ALEN *opens the door.* PAT *comes in.*

'Ow yoo keepin'? Yoo didn't expect me, did yoo?

ALEN. I didn't expect –

PAT. 'Ow yoo keepin'?

ALEN. 'Ow's I keepin'? Mustn't grumble.

PAT. That's right.

ALEN. My leg ent too good.

PAT. O.

ALEN. I still got that owd guts ache an' the pains in my back.

PAT. O.

ALEN. An' me leg.

PAT. What a shame? 'Ow are yoo?

ALEN. Mustn't grumble.

PAT. Yoo look all right.

ALEN. An' me leg.

PAT. I'll get yoo some a my linament rub for that owd back.

ALEN. My back's been playin' me up.

PAT. 'Ow doo I look?

ALEN. An' me leg.

PAT. Yoo still talk t' yoorself, then.

ALEN. What?

PAT. 'Ow yoo gettin' on with Sco?

ALEN. Eh?

PAT. Sco.

ALEN. All right.

PAT. Yoo get on all right, then.

ALEN. O yes.

PAT. 'E don't mess yoo about, doo 'e?

ALEN. No messin'.

PAT. Sure?

ALEN. What?

PAT. Is 'e regular?

ALEN. Sometime.

PAT. 'E say 'e come 'ere every other day. But yoo can't trust 'im.

ALEN. No.

PAT. Can't be trusted. (*Looks around.*) Yoo're nice an' clean, I'll
say that. 'E say 'e get a lot a overtime, late work.

ALEN. O.

PAT. 'E ent said anythin' t' yoo?

ALEN. No.

PAT. Doo 'e bring someone with 'im?

ALEN. No.

PAT. Nobody wait outside?

ALEN. No.

PAT. No one?

ALEN. Eh?

PAT. 'E ent suited a marriage.

ALEN. Eh?

PAT. Not suited for marriage.

ALEN. O.

PAT. Soon get tired. I don't see what 'e get out a it, tell yoo the truth. Yoo know.

ALEN. Yes.

PAT. Rum owd lad, ent 'e.

ALEN. Eh?

PAT. Yoo eatin'?

ALEN. All right.

PAT. Yoo eat all right?

ALEN. Yep.

PAT. Oo doo the cleanin'?

ALEN. 'E do.

PAT. Sco?

ALEN. Yep.

PAT. Doo 'e. T'ent like 'im. Won't lift a thing in my place.

ALEN. Eh?

PAT. Won't lift a thing for me.

ALEN. O.

PAT. If anyone stood outside yoo'd know.

ALEN. I'd know.

PAT. 'E ent workin' overtime where 'e work. I checked that.

ALEN. Yoo're lookin' nicely.

PAT. I arst 'em. I ent arstin' 'im, I want a find out first.

ALEN. O.

PAT. Yes.

ALEN. Swep an' wipe.

PAT. Yes. I ent stoppin' now.

ALEN. Everythin' –

PAT. I got someone waitin'. 'E get annoyed if I keep 'im standin'.

ALEN. Yoo ent gooin'?

PAT. I'll come in agen soon. Soon. I bought yoo some boil sweets. (*She hands him a small white paper bag.*) They're your favourite, ent they?

ALEN. I like boil.

PAT. I know.

ALEN. My favourite.

PAT. That's right. I'll look in agen soon's I'm down this way.

ALEN. Yes.

PAT. That's a bit out my way, see. Sure yoo got everything?

ALEN. Eh?

PAT. Good. I'm glad 'e keep yoo nice. Well, I did it for a long time, ent I?

ALEN. Long while.

PAT. I don't see why 'e can't 'elp me a bit. Yoo're on 'is way 'ome.

ALEN. Eh?

PAT. I'll 'ave t' rush. I ont tellin' 'im I arst 'bout anythin'. Doo 'e'll say I'm nosin'. I'll just say we 'ad a bit a talk.

ALEN. I –

PAT. So you behave. Yoo might get some more boil sweets.

ALEN (*he shakes the bag of sweets*). Thank yer.

PAT. That's a pleasure.

ALEN. When yoo comin' back?

PAT. Soon.

ALEN. Thank yer.

PAT. Cheerio.

   PAT *goes out through the door.*

ALEN. Thank yer. (*He bolts the door behind her. He goes to the stack of papers by the wall. He climbs on to them. He peers through a chink in the wall.*)

SCOPEY (*stands and looks at* ALEN). I never 'eard yoo talk a yoorself. Why's she say that? (*Pause.*) That what yoo use them papers for?

ALEN (*he steps down*). She's on a bike.

SCOPEY. O.

ALEN. Peddled off like the devil after 'er. Roads ent safe.

SCOPEY. Yoo was glad a see 'er.

ALEN. She look all right.

SCOPEY. I thought so.

ALEN. Eh?

SCOPEY. Yoo was glad a see 'er.

ALEN. She say she's comin' back regular.

SCOPEY. That's what you want.

ALEN. I like gals.

SCOPEY. Chriss!

ALEN. When she comin' back?

SCOPEY. I got the sack t'day.

ALEN. O.

SCOPEY. That's count a spendin' too much time 'ere when I should a been a work.

ALEN. That ent my fault.

SCOPEY. I never said it was.

ALEN. Yoo ont get no money out a me.

SCOPEY. I never arst for money!

ALEN. I ont got it.

SCOPEY. I don't want it! Stick it!

ALEN. Eh?

SCOPEY. Yoo'll see if she come back! I'll arst 'er!

ALEN. Yoo gooin' a arst 'er?

SCOPEY. She'll laugh 'er 'ead off.

ALEN. She came a see me.

SCOPEY. Snoopin'. That's all she's after. Chriss, yoo don't know anythin'.

ALEN. What?

SCOPEY. In the war they reckon yoo was flashin' secrets a the jerries with a Woolworth's torch. Yoo couldn't even light a cigarette.

ALEN. Tobacco an' drink are Satan's whores.

SCOPEY. Yoo owd nut! I thought yoo 'ad them papers for keepin'. All yoo want 'em for's t' stare outside. Yoo owd fake!

ALEN. No.

SCOPEY. All day!

ALEN. Don't row at me!

SCOPEY. Don't yoo? Yoo're at that crack all day! Starin' out! It all goos on outside an' yoo just watch!

ALEN. I ont said I –

SCOPEY. Yoo're a fake! There's nothin' in this bloody shop!

ALEN. My little jobs –

SCOPEY. Jobs! Starin' out! Talk t' yourself! I 'eard! What for?

ALEN. No.

SCOPEY. What about? What yoo talk about? Nothin'!

ALEN. No. No.

SCOPEY. What about?

ALEN. Not my –

SCOPEY. Let's 'ear yoo! Goo on – talk! Drivel!

ALEN. Stop!

SCOPEY. Talk!

ALEN. She lied to –

SCOPEY. Liar!

ALEN. I sing sometime.

SCOPEY. Sing?

ALEN. Sometime.

SCOPEY. All right –

ALEN. No.

SCOPEY. Sing! What sort a singing? What sort a songs?

ALEN. Hymns.

SCOPEY. Sing a hymn.

ALEN. No.

SCOPEY. Sing it mate! Sing it. By chriss I'll rip this junk shop up
 if yoo don't sing! (*He puts his boot through the couch.*)

ALEN (*he starts to sing. At first he wavers, but the rhythm controls
 his terror*).

>   Little babe nailed to the tree
>   Wash our souls in thy pure blood
>   Cleanse each sin and let us be
>   Baptized in the purple flood
>
>   Bearing thorns and whips and nails
>   Wise men kneel before thy bier
>   Let the love that never fails
>   Conquer vice and death and fear

Child thy hosts now crowd the sky
Thou who found love here alone
Those who nail thee up to die
Hoist thee nearer to thy throne

(*Pause.*) Amen. (*Pause.*) I ent sure a the words. I used a follow the service on my wireless set but on the last war Mr Lowerly started up rumours count I owed 'im five an' six for milk bill an' the police come up an' took my wireless set so's I couldn't 'ear Lord Haw-Haw, so 'e say.

SCOPEY. God, 'alf the junk in 'ere could be burnt. Yoo don't need it. Look. (*Slight pause.*) What yoo 'ere for?

ALEN. I forget.

SCOPEY. Look at it! For chriss sake try t' tell the truth!

ALEN. I forget. My mum an' dad moved all over. We always stopped just outside places. We were the last 'ouse in the village.

SCOPEY. How?

ALEN. Yes.

SCOPEY. *How?*

ALEN. I never stopped gooin' after people. They stopped gooin' after me.

SCOPEY. I don't believe that.

ALEN. That's all I can bring back. (*Pause.*) Yoo arstin' 'er t' come?

SCOPEY (*after a pause*). Pockets're empty.

ALEN. Sew them back.

    SCOPEY *looks down at the hole in the bed.*

That keeps the owd shape, else that don't look nothin'.

    SCOPEY *sits on the bed with the coat.*

Scene Thirteen

An open space. An iron railing up stage centre. This is used for leaning against.

JUNE, JOE *and* RON *come in from the left.* JUNE *and* JOE *hold hands.*

JUNE. Saw telly last night. Pat come round my place agen.

JOE. Good?

JUNE. Boxin'.

JOE. All right?

JUNE. Why ent they allowed a wear white shorts?

JOE. Eh?

JUNE. Why can't they wear white shorts?

JOE. Don't know.

RON. Count a they'd show the blood.

JUNE. I 'eard it's so's yoo can't see what they got underneath when it get all sweaty. (*She giggles.*)

JOE. It's traditional.

RON. Where they two got to? (*He looks off left.*)

JUNE. They're all right. Leave 'em alone.

JOE. No, let 'em catch up.

JUNE. Can't miss nothin', can yoo.

RON. She off t' owd boy Alen's?

JUNE. She don't goo round there.

RON. Why's that?

JUNE. Scopey doo that for 'er.

JOE. 'E say 'e couldn't stand the owd bastard.

JUNE. Well, that's on 'is way 'ome.

JOE. Doo 'e doo the washin' up for 'er?

> JOE *and* RON *laugh.*

JOE. Let's goo there one night an' sort the owd sod out.

JUNE. No yoo ent.

RON. Just for a laugh.

JUNE. 'E ent 'urt yoo.

JOE. Yoo can come.

JUNE. What doo I want to come for? Yoo goo givin' shocks to an owd boy that age and yoo might be sorry.

JOE. Don't be daft.

RON. Just for a laugh.

JUNE. Yoo'll land yourself into trouble, boy.

> BILL *and* PAT *come in from the left.*

JUNE. Why ent boxers allowed a wear white shorts?

BILL. So's yoo can see when they get 'it low.

JUNE. There was a lot a that last night.

PAT. I felt sorry for that dark fella.

JUNE. Shouldn't come over 'ere.

PAT. Blood everywhere. Must a got splashed if yoo was sittin' close. Waste.

JUNE. What is?

PAT. That blood?

RON. Why?

PAT. They could use that in 'ospitals.

BILL. They got plenty.

JOE. If yoo give it, they never pay.

RON. Somethin' for nothin'.

JOE. They come round the TA once. Lousy tea an' a dog biscuit. I said no.

RON. I smoke 'eavy, so they won't touch mine.

JOE. We're gooin' down the Carpenter's.

BILL. Comin'.

PAT. Yeh, I ent 'ad a drink for a long while.

RON. Sco 'ome?

PAT. Don't know.

JUNE. 'E never know when 'e'll be in.

BILL. Got a fag?

    RON *gives him one.*

  Ta.

JUNE. Most likely still up owd Alen's.

PAT. I don't think I'll come.

BILL. Make up yoor mind, gal.

PAT. No, I won't, thanks.

JUNE. Yoo come, love.

PAT. No.

BILL. Up t' yoo?

RON. Yoo payin' then?

BILL. I'll see yoo 'ome.

PAT. Ta.

JOE. Be in for a quick one later?

BILL. Sure.

RON. I'll 'ave it on the bar waitin'.

BILL. Better be the best.

    BILL *and* PAT *go out right.*

Scene Fourteen

ALEN's *place.*

There are seven or eight tins of food on the table. One of them has been opened. Down left there is a bundle on the floor.

SCOPEY *stands up right on the pile of papers. He wears his greatcoat. He steps down and picks up the broom. He sweeps. The head comes off the broom. He stoops. He picks the head up. He pulls fluff from the bristles. He drops the fluff on the floor. He sits on the edge of the couch. He makes a wedge from paper and stuffs it in the hole in the broom head. He screws in the broom handle. He lays the broom on the couch. He pulls at the covers with one hand. Pause. He looks up – his head is held stiff. He listens. Pause. He drops his head to just below the normal position, pulling his neck into his shoulders, his chin horizontal. He shivers. He takes up the broom. He screws the handle tighter. He stands. He puts the broom back on the bed. He goes to the burners. He takes out a large watch from inside his coat. He looks at it. He shakes it. He puts it to his ear. He goes to the table and takes a knife from the drawer. He leaves the drawer open and goes back to the burners. He tries to open the watch with the knife. He can't. He sits on a box. He shakes the watch.*

VOICES (*off*).

> I love my babee
> I love her real good
> Love her day and night
> Like a lover should.

I love my babee
I squeeze her real tight
Love her all the day
Till its broad daylight.

RON (*off. Sings*). Drop your drawers, I'm comin' down the chimney.

BYO (*off*). Number two on the Brylcream.

A stone strikes the wall.

BYO (*off*). Open up, boy.

LORRY (*off*). Kick the bleedin' door in.

VOICES (*off*).

While shepherds watch their flocks by night
A whore lay in the grass
The angel of the Lord came down
And stuck it up her pass the mustard share the salt.
The Lord above is kind
And if yoo thought of something else
You've got a dirty arse.

LEN (*off*). Open up, yoo owd bastard.

RON (*off*). Let's 'ave a look at yoo.

A stone strikes the wall.

JUNE (*off*). Oo's got the matches?

BYO (*after a silence*). Oo yoo got in there, boy?

JOE (*off*). We're comin' down the roof.

JUNE (*off*). Oo's been interferin' with little gals?

RON (*off*). What about that little gal at Finchin?

BYO (*off*). An the boys.

RON (*off*). What yoo got a 'ide for?

JUNE (*off*). Shut up!

BYO (*off*). What?

JUNE (*off*). Listen!

RON (*after a pause. Off*). What?

JUNE (*off*). I 'eard 'im.

Screams. Laughs. The noise of tins being banged.

BYO (*off*). Perhaps 'e's poopin'.

RON (*off*). Do 'e sit on a po?

JUNE (*off*). Got any paper?

Laughs. Shouts. Stones strike the wall.

RON (*off*). Bastard!

BYO (*off*). Lousy bastard!

JOE (*off*). Rotten bastard!

LEN (*off*). Stinkin' bastard!

RON (*off*). Bastard bastard!

JUNE (*off*). Come yoo 'ere and interfere with me!

Shrieks. Laughs.

JOE (*off*). 'E only like 'em young.

JUNE (*off*). Cheeky bastard!

Shrieks. Laughs.

JUNE (*off*). Stop it! (*She screams.*)

BYO (*off*). Put your boy scout 'at on an' come an' save 'er.

RON (*off*). She's bein' raped.

BYO (*off*). Don't shove till yoor 'ead a the queue.

JUNE (*off*). Next please.

JOE (*off*). I'm on t' a good thing 'ere. I reckon I'll put 'er up in the business.

Laughs. Shouts. A shower of stones strike the wall.

BYO (*off*). The owd sod's asleep.

JUNE (*off*). Come an' buy me a drink, lovie.

JOE (*off*). 'E's put 'is curse on yoo!

BYO *makes ghost noises. Noise of tins being struck.* JUNE *shrieks.*

BYO (*off*). 'E'll come an' 'aunt yoo.

JUNE (*off*). I'm off!

Slight silence. A few stones strike the wall.

JUNE (*farther off*). Byo Luke's pissin' on yoor door.

BYO (*off*). Bring out yoor dead!

A solitary can is struck. Slight silence. A stone strikes the wall. Laughs. Shouts.

RON (*farther off*). We're gooin' a watch yoo, mate.

BYO (*off*). Red!

RON (*farther off*). See if yoo can 'it that door from 'ere.

Slight pause. A stone hits the wall. Distant shouts. Three stones hit the wall. Distant shouts. Pause. One very distant shout. Silence.

SCOPEY *sits.*

Scene Fifteen

SCOPEY *and* PAT's *place.*
BILL *sits at the table.* PAT *is behind him. She straightens her stocking.*

BILL. Chriss I'm stiff.

PAT. Stiff?

BILL. Yep.

PAT. Ent surprisin'.

BILL. Feel more like gooin' a bed than drinkin'.

PAT. Ooo yoo kiddin'?

BILL. Straight.

PAT. You'd live in the owd pub if yoo won the pools.

BILL (*stretches*). They'd a been lost without owd man Bullright.

PAT. Kill 'imself. Gaddin' bout 'is age.

BILL. I know I'm stiff. Yoo'll 'ave t' doo your stuff, gal.

PAT. I'll rub some a my rub on that latter, but that ont doo now doo yoo'll get stain all over yoor cloths.

BILL. That's a deal. Ent yoo ready yet, gal?

PAT. What about Sco?

BILL. Well?

PAT. I ought a howd on a bit longer, b'rights.

BILL. Did 'e say when 'e'd get back?

PAT. Yo know 'e don't.

BILL. That's that then.

    PAT *goes off right.* BILL *lights a cigarette.*

I reckon 'e's got 'imself fixed up with some piece.

PAT (*off*). What?

BILL. I reckon 'e's gettin' it outside.

PAT (*off*). No. (*Pause.*) 'Oo?

BILL. Anyone.

PAT (*off*). No. (*Slight pause.*) That'd soon get back a me.

BILL. Well 'e must be gettin' it some place.

PAT *comes in from the right.*

PAT. All right?

BILL. Very nice.

PAT (*wiping her hands on a towel*). 'E ent give me my money this week. (*Pause.*) I don't like gooin' in pubs with an empty purse.

BILL. 'Ow much?

PAT. Don't bother. I'll settle up with 'im.

BILL. I 'ont 'angin' round 'ere all day. (*Pause.*) Comin' in a Stor'ford Saturday? I'm puttin' the deposit down on my new car.

PAT. That sounds nice.

BILL. Comin'?

PAT. Sure. (*She looks at him.*) Don't seem like a year since I been married, doo it.

BILL. No.

PAT. I 'ave.

BILL. 'Urry up.

PAT. Don't shout.

PAT *goes off right. Sound of water running in a basin. Pause.* SCOPEY *wheels in his bike from left and crosses the back stage. He leans his bike against the centre of the back stage wall. He comes down.*

BILL. 'Ow yoo dooin', boy?

SCOPEY. Fine.

BILL. Nice t' see yoo.

SCOPEY. 'Ow're yoo?

BILL. Usual.

SCOPEY. Busy?

BILL. Yep.

SCOPEY. Ha.

BILL. Where yoo tore yoor pants?

SCOPEY. O.

BILL. By the side.

SCOPEY. That owd bike.

BILL. Yoo can 'ave mine for a fiver. I want a get rid a it.

SCOPEY. No thanks.

BILL. Worth more. That's a good owd bike.

> PAT *comes in from right.*

PAT. We're gooin' down the pub.

BILL. Yoo comin'?

SCOPEY. Yoo ready?

PAT. Yep.

SCOPEY. I need a clean up.

PAT. That 'ont take yoo long.

SCOPEY. I 'eard the result.

BILL. Yoo should a see owd man Bullright. That's 'is last game,
yoo know.

SCOPEY. I 'eard tell.

BILL. Official – or 'e say. I don't reckon they'll ever get anyone a
send 'em down like 'e did. We could a used yoo. Pity.

SCOPEY. That's ow it goo.

BILL. Yup. The lads arst after yoo.

PAT. We'll 'e'll see 'imself tonight.

BILL. Sure. Nice 'avin' all the crowd t'gether agen.

PAT. I need some money.

SCOPEY. Now?

PAT. Yeh.

SCOPEY. Not now. I got a get cleaned up.

PAT. I'm gooin' a get it settled afore I set foot out a this 'ouse.

SCOPEY. Sure. Well I'll get my jacket. (*He goes up to his bike and
takes his jacket from the handlebars.*)

PAT. 'Ow long yoo gooin' a be?

SCOPEY. Don't know, dear.

PAT. Shall we wait?

SCOPEY. Yoo goo on an' I'll join yoo.

PAT. Where yoo been?

SCOPEY. I come's fast I could. (*He comes down with the jacket. He is searching through the pockets.*)

PAT. Look in on the owd boy?

SCOPEY. Yup.

BILL. 'Ow's the job?

SCOPEY. All right.

BILL. When yoo start bringin' it in?

SCOPEY. Anytime, I reckon.

PAT. What's the matter?

SCOPEY (*going through the pockets again*). I can't recollect where I put it.

PAT. I ent touchin' my money. That's for the hp.

SCOPEY. Ooo arst yoo a touch it?

    BILL *stands*.

PAT. Don't be daft, boy. Sit yoo down.

BILL. They're all gettin' a start on us. There won't be none left.

PAT. Well?

SCOPEY (*putting packet on a chair*). I'll sort it out later. I ont dooin' nothin' till I 'ad my wash. I feel all grit.

PAT. Bill, lend me a quid.

BILL (*embarrassed*). All right, all right.

PAT. Now, please.

BILL. What's the matter with yoo?

PAT. I 'ont let both a yoo let me down.

BILL. All right. (*He quickly hands over a pound note. He tries not to let the paper show, but* PAT *flicks it noisily.*)

SCOPEY. Oo's lettin' you down?

PAT. Where yoo been?

SCOPEY. Eh?

PAT. Where yoo been?

SCOPEY. I told yoo. Ta, Bill. I'll pay you back soon's I –

PAT. Yoo never told me. Yoo said yoo –

BILL. We gooin' or ent we?

PAT. All right!

SCOPEY (*after a pause*). I'll buy the owd boy's grub after today.

PAT. Yoo still owe me for the last two weeks. (*She puts cosmetics into her handbag.*) I'll come round there an collect it myself after this. I can't afford a feed 'im. Yoo get 'is grub! If I relied on yoo 'e'd starve.

PAT *goes out right. Pause.*

SCOPEY. D'yoo 'ave anythin' t' eat?

BILL. Sandwich.

SCOPEY. That enough?

BILL. 'Ave t' leave a hole for the beer.

SCOPEY. Yeh.

BILL. What we gooin' a doo?

SCOPEY. Yoo take 'er an' I'll join yoo soon's I can.

BILL. Sure?

SCOPEY. Yeh.

BILL. Well don't forget, boy. I'll buy yoo a short for owd times.

SCOPEY. Sounds all right.

PAT *comes in from the right.*

PAT. Ready?

BILL. I been ready 'ours.

PAT. We're off. (*She takes her bag from the table.*)

BILL. See yer.

SCOPEY. Yup.

PAT. Don't be late.

SCOPEY. No.

PAT *and* BILL *go out right.*

SCOPEY *goes to the table. He stands and cuts a slice of bread. He butters it. He eats. He sits. He takes a second mouthful. He chews it monotonously. He stops. He chews again. He swallows. He stands. He unbuttons the front of his shirt. He pours a cup of tea, after feeling that the teapot is hot. He adds milk. He drinks. He puts the cup back on the table. He unfastens the cuffs of his shirt. He picks up the loaf and butter. He goes out right. Slight pause. The noise of running water. He comes back. He picks up the cup and saucer. He starts to go right. He hesitates. He stops.*

He stares at the cup and saucer for a long time. Nothing moves.
Slowly he turns. He puts the cup and saucer back on the table.
He wanders a few steps down right. He turns and pushes the chair
under the table. He fastens his cuffs and front. He picks up his
jacket.
He goes out right. The running water stops. Noise of water
being thrown away. He comes back. He scoops up some papers
bundled on the floor. He goes up to his bike. He throws his jacket
over the handlebars. He wheels it off left.

Scene Sixteen

ALEN's *place.*
SCOPEY *sits down stage slightly left on a box. He wears his greatcoat.*
There are five hundred tins of food on the table and floor. They are
heaped round SCOPEY *and the bundle down left. Only five of the*
tins have been opened.
Pause.
The door opens. PAT *comes in. She wears an old white mack. The*
cuffs, collar and hem are dirty grey. She wears on her head a dingy
white and red scarf.

PAT. Hello. (*She comes down towards* SCOPEY.) Where's the owd
    boy? (*She looks at the tins.*) Scopey? (*She sees the bundle on the*
    floor and starts to go to it.)
SCOPEY. I 'oisted the flap a month back. 'Is 'ead's like a fish.
PAT. 'E's dead.
SCOPEY. All silver scales.
PAT. Why 'ent yoo come?
SCOPEY. I took one 'and on 'is throat an one 'eld 'im up be the 'air.
PAT. Why?
SCOPEY. One 'and.
PAT. That's 'is coat.
SCOPEY. I stole it.
PAT. They'll 'ang you.

SCOPEY. One be the 'air.

PAT. Stay there. (*She goes up to the door.*) I 'ont be far. (*She goes out. Off.*) Bill! Bill!

BILL (*far off*). What?

PAT (*off*). 'Elp!

    SCOPEY *sits.*

Stories

MR DOG

The old lady who lives opposite me has long white hair, warts and talks to her dog. Three hundred years ago she would have been burned for a witch – I live in East Anglia, witch-burning country. Her house stands away from the road at the back of a big garden. It is a wilderness with patches in it. She does a lot of gardening, but she is eighty-four and she can only cultivate a few patches.

When I walk by her house her dog comes out of its kennel and stands on top of it, and watches me with its ears and its tail up, and I can hear the chain slithering over the kennel. It lives on this chain, and two times a day she takes it off the chain and puts it on a lead and takes it for a walk. It gets its walk even when it snows.

Last summer when they cut the corn in the field at the side of the house, I remember, they were shooting rabbits in the stubble. Three men stood in the field with rifles at their shoulders, very stiff, like toy soldiers. They waited and when a rabbit ran they swung their rifles after it and fired. The rabbit was often knocked two or three feet off the ground. The boys, helping the men, would zig-zag after it and pick it up by the hind legs. It writhed in the air and they hit it on the head with a long thin stone – like a short rolling pin – and it suddenly went still.

They came off the field and stopped to say 'Evening'. They stood by my gate and all of them had bunches of rabbits hanging from both hands. My dog put its head through the gate bars and sniffed. One of the rabbits was partly alive, or moving while dead, and it kept jerking its head and looking round and then up at its own body. My dog stared at the jerking head and gave a high whine.

They shoot dogs if they kill chickens. My dog gets out and I suppose she kills chickens and perhaps they'll shoot her one day. I can see how it would happen. The first bullet would plough a pink furrow across her back and she would jump into the air in pain and surprise and spin round. The second would go into her shoulder while she was in the air and she would fall down on the ground and stare at the farmer coming towards her. The third shot would go into her head.

The other day I took my dog along the bridle path to the village common. She sniffed and ran ahead and went out of sight round a corner and I heard barking and shouting. I ran round the corner and saw the old woman pulling her dog towards her by the lead, and with her free hand she was hitting it across the back with a walking-stick. The dog didn't notice it was being hit; it yelped and strained at my dog, which was crouching in the grass and yelping back.

The old woman said, 'I never knew 'er goo for another dog before. But bitch will goo for bitch.'

My dog darted a few feet away and I saw blood between its back legs. For a second I was puzzled but then I saw that her tail had been bitten, and the blood must have smeared when she crouched in the grass with her tail between her legs.

I bent down towards the old woman's dog and put out a hand to touch it. It stared at me. Its ears and tail were rigidly alert, its brown hair bristled and glistened, and it stood with its feet wide apart, firmly and tensely, and its head lifted up and back at an inquisitive angle. Its mouth was a bit open but it didn't move – the whole dog was still – and its bright eyes were turned slightly to the left to look straight at me, and as I looked at its eyes I saw at once that it was lunatic. It was not berserk mad, but lunatic, like people you see in a mad-house who stand still all day with empty shopping baskets and stare straight ahead of them. They live in a state of surprise, but surprise without tension – because the surprise has lasted so long. So the dog was totally lunatic, but still gentle; and my dog coming tearing up to play had frightened it.

The old woman said 'Never knewd it' several times and dropped the lead. She made a little frightened sound, and I picked it up for her, but the movement frightened the dog and it pulled away and I felt the wet leather lead slither through my hand. But the dog stopped. Perhaps it was puzzled because it couldn't feel the weight of the kennel or the old woman on the end of the lead.

Then I remembered that I had often heard the dog yelping for hours at a time and at first I'd thought it was when the old woman had gone out. But then I'd noticed it wasn't. The dog just used to climb on top of its kennel and yelp, and in time this became a habit and it wasn't yelping *at* anything but just yelping. It had gone lunatic.

The old woman took the lead and thanked me and went down the path with her dog.

THE KING WITH GOLDEN EYES

There was a wise old man who had golden eyes. He left them in his will to a surgeon. He died. On the day the surgeon got the golden eyes his wife had a son. The surgeon said, 'I'll give the golden eyes to my son. They will make him famous and powerful.' He took out the child's eyes and put the golden eyes in their place. And the surgeon was right: everyone worshipped the child because of his magic eyes, and they did everything for him. They carried him about, fed him, worked for him, entertained him, fell in love with him, obeyed him, fought for him. He became king. He married a princess with a beautiful voice. He became very powerful and his kingdom got bigger and bigger. He ruled all he could have surveyed if he hadn't been blind. He would have liked to see his kingdom and all his soldiers and the crowds cheering him. As he was now very rich he opened an academy. He brought scientists from all over the world and told them they were to study his blindness and make him see. They thought and experimented. They did lots of things to the eyes of dogs and cats and rats. They could make them blind but they couldn't make them see. In the end they decided the king would have to be fitted with the eyes of a child, because he had lost his eyes when he was a child. They took the eyes from a very little child and fitted them into the king. They did this in a dark room because suddenly seeing the light might blind the king again. Then they took him through his palace. Each room they went in was a bit lighter than the one before. The first room was very dim, but at the end they led the king out on to the steps of his garden, and the king saw the brilliant light. He was dazzled and happy. He said, 'Now I shall be a greater king than ever! Because I can see! When I try prisoners I will tell from their faces which are guilty! And I can fight my war better, because I shall see the enemy positions at a glance and send my soldiers into battle quicker!'

They brought him a man who'd stolen a chicken and eaten it. They knew he'd done this because lots of people had seen him. The king heard the evidence and then looked at the man. But he was confused. The man didn't look guilty. So he said, 'I shall go to my private room and think about this.' All the witnesses and officials waited in the court. They were a bit gloomy because they wanted to go home, but the king had to think about the puzzling thing he'd seen. He spent all day puzzling about it. He couldn't make up his mind.

The next day the generals came to see him. They shewed him a map and they marked on it where the enemy were hiding. The king pointed and said, 'Send some men along the river and tell the others to hide there,' and he pointed at a forest. The generals did this with the soldiers and they won a great victory and captured a new city. The king went to see his new city. On the way there he kept puzzling about the thief who didn't look guilty. He was very pleased with his new city. On the way back he was still puzzling about the thief. He decided not to try any more cases.

That night he had his first dream. He hadn't dreamed before, because, being blind, he didn't know how to see things when he was asleep. He dreamed about the thief. The thief was an old beggar. In the dream he knelt and held out his hands. The king noticed they were dirty. He put a coin into the beggar's hands. The beggar turned into a judge.

In the morning the king went to court. He told the officials and soldiers to let the thief go. The woman who'd lost the chicken complained. But the king insisted. So the prisoner was let out and he went away. The woman went home, still complaining. Everyone was worried because they knew that the thief had taken the chicken. He'd been seen. They said, 'Now people will take what they want. No one will be safe.' In the morning all the people came to the palace and complained. They were very worried because they'd trusted their king and he'd never done anything wrong before. They said, 'Condemn the thief!' The king said,

'He's not guilty. I've looked at his face.' The people were angry and they wouldn't go away.

The generals came to see the king. The people in the new city had armed themselves and were going to fight the king's soldiers. But the generals couldn't get near the palace because all the people were crowded there. In the afternoon the people from the king's new city attacked the king's soldiers. The king hadn't told the generals where to put the soldiers so the soldiers were defeated. That evening they came home and the people saw them. They had cuts and other wounds, some of them shouted and cried, some had lost legs and arms, some had to be carried, some were lying dead in a cart. The people were very angry when they saw this. Their soldiers hadn't been defeated before. The king came out on to the balcony to look at his soldiers. The people stared at him. After a time he went back into the palace. The people said, 'He's just an ordinary man, really. He's lost his magic golden eyes.' They shouted to the king to put back his golden eyes. The king said 'No'. The ministers pleaded with him. They even went on to their knees. But the king said 'No'. Finally, when it was dark, the people got very angry. They attacked the palace and set parts of it on fire. The soldiers wouldn't defend the king. They were angry because they'd been wounded and defeated. The ministers wouldn't support him because he wouldn't do what was necessary and put back his golden eyes. So the king had to leave the palace. He slipped out quickly in the dark. He walked away from the city and kept on walking all night. When it began to get light he was in the country. He looked behind but he'd walked so far he couldn't see the city.

After some time he was walking along the bank of a river. He saw an old man cutting reeds but the king didn't stop to talk to him. Farther on he came to a child. The child was sitting by the edge of the river. The king was surprised to see the child had no eyes. The king said, 'This must be the child whose eyes they gave to me.' So the king said, 'Come with me and I will guide you and take care of you.' The child stood up and started to walk along beside the king. Again the king was surprised because the child walked as if he could see where he was going. The king looked at the child's face and saw water running down his cheeks. He said, 'What is that?' and the child said 'Tears'. The king was surprised. He'd never seen tears before and he'd never cried with his new eyes. The king looked closely at the tears, and then he saw a really astonishing thing. Each tear falling down the child's face was an eye. The king said to himself 'This child can see everything' and he saw that the little eyes covered the child's body and even dripped from the ends of his fingers. There were long streaks of eyes on the ground, running from the child to the river. They glittered in the light. The king looked at the river and said that that was made of tears, too, glittering in the light.

SHARPEVILLE SEQUENCE

A Scene, a Story and Three Poems

(Written for the Sharpeville Massacre Tenth Anniversary Commemoration Evening, held by the Anti-Apartheid Movement at the Lyceum Theatre on March 22, 1970).

Poem: I Cannot Mourn

I cannot mourn men killed at Sharpeville
How can I mourn when I have to say who are they?
Faces I have not seen, unrecognizable in dust anyway
Voices I have not heard, the screams could be anyone's
Hands fighting death, making gestures you see on posters
How can I mourn when I can't believe it happened?
How can I believe men shot parents running to hold their
[children?
How can I believe men shot children?
What men shoot children in the back?

But I can understand when I see it like this
Sharpeville isn't a village
It isn't even a nation
It's an effect that follows a cause
Be afraid like that
Covet like that
Hate like that
Believe in the armed state
That is the font of all wisdom and violence
And the effect follows
Sharpeville is very simple

The sentry must challenge the dark and shoot the mountain
The righteous must have their victim

Then the bodies are stacked by my door
I step over them in the street when I go home
I wake and they're piled at my window

Scene: Black Mass

*A church at Vereeniging. An altar and a large cross. The altar is
plain and covered by a white cloth. The cross is made of simple wood.
A lifesize Christ is nailed to it. A* PRIEST *and a* PRIME MINISTER.
The PRIME MINISTER *kneels for communion.*

PRIEST. Ye that do truly and earnestly repent you of your sins and
are in love and charity with your neighbours and intend to lead
a new life make your humble confession to almighty god meekly
kneeling upon your knees. (*Pause.*) Meekly kneeling upon your
knees . . .

PRIME MINISTER (*after a pause*). You said something, padre?

PRIEST. You have a lot on your mind.

PRIME MINISTER. True.

PRIEST. Something in particular, prime minister? Perhaps I can
help.

PRIME MINISTER. You are a help, padre. It's nothing in particular. I wish – I wish I got a little more understanding. Something more in the way of appreciation. Even a bit less abuse.
But you know, padre, I tell myself – I only tell myself in secret,
of course – that men of vision are bound to be misunderstood in
their own time and being misunderstood is part of the privilege
of being a man of vision. Well, let's get on. There's a cabinet
meeting this afternoon. You were saying?

PRIEST. Meekly kneeling upon your knees.

PRIME MINISTER. Ah, yes. Almighty god judge of all men we
acknowledge and bewail our manifold sins and wickednesses

which we – and now there's that crowd of Kaffirs down the road
– from time to time most grievously have committed by thought
word and deed – just stuck there – we do earnestly repent and
are heartily sorry for these our misdoings the remembrance of
them is grievous unto us the burden of them intolerable have
mercy upon us – you'd think they'd have the decency to go,
they get pleasure out of causing trouble and giving me a bad
name abroad – padre, yes, have mercy upon us – and what can
I do, they tie my hands and stand in front of the gun and when
I squeeze the trigger it's my fault because they're aggressive
enough to get hit, I must make a note of that for the cabinet
meeting (*he writes in a little notebook*) – did I say we acknowledge
and bewail our manifold – note how I'm on my knees, I wish
they could see that abroad, I'm not ashamed to pray for
guidance, how else could I be sure I was doing the right thing? –
But I mustn't stay here talking, padre, enjoyable though that is.
We must put our hand to the plow, amen.

PRIEST. Lift up your hearts.

PRIME MINISTER. We lift them up.

> *An* INSPECTOR *comes in. The* PRIEST *goes to the altar and
> prepares communion.*

INSPECTOR. The Kaffirs are still there, sir.

PRIME MINISTER. You showed them the planes?

INSPECTOR. Did do, sir.

PRIME MINISTER. And they still stayed?

INSPECTOR. So we brought in reinforcements. The lads didn't
like it. They were playing rugger, tennis, cricket, and other
mind-cleansing and body-building games, but they came when
they heard the summons.

PRIME MINISTER. What about the Saracens?

INSPECTOR. As useless as the planes.

PRIME MINISTER. Oh.

INSPECTOR. They're British made, so you wouldn't expect them
to work. You might as well send them out on the milk round.
Never mind, we've got our own personal weapons, all made in

the home country – they'll shift them. (*He goes to the altar, where the* PRIEST *is making ritual gestures.*) Could I disturb you for a moment, padre? (*He takes rifles from under the altar.*) Could you say a prayer for the boys while you're at it, padre?

PRIEST. I'm always praying for the boys.

INSPECTOR. Thank you padre. We'll do you a good turn some-day, man.

> *The* INSPECTOR *leaves. The* PRIEST *turns to the* PRIME MINISTER *with the bread and wine.*

PRIME MINISTER. Time spent on your knees is never wasted.

PRIEST. I wish more people thought like you, prime minister.

PRIME MINISTER. So do I.

PRIEST (*offering the bread*). Take and eat this in remembrance that christ died for thee and feed on him –

> *Loud rifle fire, off. After twenty seconds the* PRIEST *speaks again.*

PRIEST. Do you hear a noise, prime minister?

PRIME MINISTER. No.

PRIEST. I think perhaps there *is* a sound. Perhaps we should go and see if we can –

PRIME MINISTER. I don't know what you hear, but I can't hear it. *My* mind is entirely concentrated on the appropriate holy thoughts.

PRIEST. Oh so is mine! But I thought I – well, your hearing is better than mine.

PRIME MINISTER. Then let's get on. I can't keep the cabinet waiting.

> *The rifle fire stops and the* INSPECTOR *comes in.*

INSPECTOR. We had to use fire, sir.

PRIME MINISTER. Dear me.

INSPECTOR. They wouldn't go. And the lads were impatient. They'd been pulled away in the middle of their matches, you see, sir – naturally they were keen to get back and win! There's no fun in shooting at people nowadays. Too many rules in the game. It doesn't really qualify as a sport any more – though

mind you the lads still try to play in the spirit of the old ama-
teurs, even if they've turned professional. But it can't hold a
candle to wildfowling. You've shot one man and you've shot
them all. Still, they put up a show.

PRIME MINISTER. What was the final score?

INSPECTOR. 69–0. They certainly didn't let the opposition walk
over them. The lads really put their backs into the training.
There *were* a few they could have brought off if they'd been on
the ball. They set them up, but they couldn't follow it through.
Still, they showed real style and you can't ask fairer than that.
They've gone off to the shower. Might be as well if you had a
word with them, sir. After all, they won. They're good lads and
I don't doubt for one moment they're their own hardest critics.
I watched their faces and you could see how when one of them
missed he knew he'd let the team down. The lady folk have
prepared some beer and sandwiches and a few party dainties –
perhaps you'd care to join us, padre?

PRIEST. Later on, I'd like that.

PRIME MINISTER. We'll just give them a pat on the head now,
while they're hosing down. They like to see the board going
round straight after the whistle – show them you take an interest.

The PRIME MINISTER, INSPECTOR *and* PRIEST *go.* CHRIST
*comes down from the cross. He raises his hands to speak, but
drops them. He puts something in the communion wine, and goes
back on to the cross. The* PRIME MINISTER *and* PRIEST *return.*

PRIEST. Most of them were shot in the back.

PRIME MINISTER (*kneeling*). It's the nature of the Kaffir to turn
his back when confronted with the white man's weapons.

PRIEST. Shall we finish this?

PRIME MINISTER. It's a long day but it has its rewards.

PRIEST (*offers bread*). Take this and remember that Christ died
for thee.

PRIME MINISTER (*swallows*). You know, the lads think it's all
over now and they can go home and sleep quietly in their beds
like little children, but I'll be burning the midnight oil – the

paperwork a thing like this involves – the paperwork – it never stops! I only wish you could dispose of paper as easily as you dispose of people. Paper's more difficult to handle.

PRIEST (*offers wine*). Drink this in remembrance that christ's blood was shed for thee and be thankful.

PRIME MINISTER. I don't begrudge them their sleep when they've earned it – but there are times when I could gladly lay down the burdens of the helm. (*Dies.*)

The INSPECTOR *comes in.*

INSPECTOR. Did I hear a body falling? Too late! I shall examine the scene of the crime for clues and pounce on the accused with professional speed. Note how, as he faced his maker, he showed the whites of his eyes.

PRIEST. I wish it could have happened somewhere else. It looks bad here.

INSPECTOR. That's the mark of the black hand – no respect for the proprieties. This is a typical Kaffir foul – behind the umpire's back. I'm on to something here! A row of little spots. The accused was crying – unless I'm mistaken and he was peeing himself.

PRIEST. In church?

INSPECTOR. Just a little joke, padre. No intention of mocking the cloth. (*He follows the trail of spots to the cross.*) And here we have just what I was looking for: a little puddle. (*To* CHRIST.) Just a moment, sir. (*Takes out a notebook.*) Would you mind telling me your name, permanent address and occupation and explain what you're doing trespassing on these premises?

PRIEST. I think there's a mistake, Inspector.

INSPECTOR. You know this fellow, sir?

PRIEST. Yes.

INSPECTOR (*starts to put his notebook away*). In that case I take it you're not prepared to vouch for this gentleman's bona fides.

PRIEST. Well . . . not entirely.

INSPECTOR. I see. Dearie me then. In that case I must ask the gentleman to accompany me to the station.

H

PRIEST. No. I – let me pray for guidance.

INSPECTOR. In the circumstances I think prayer comes under the Conspiracy Act.

PRIEST. That makes it difficult. I'll have to guess the answer. (*To* CHRIST.) I'm afraid I must ask you to leave.

INSPECTOR. I'm sorry, padre. It's gone further than that.

PRIEST. This is the best way. The whole incident could be blown up out of proportion.

INSPECTOR. You mean the gentleman has friends abroad?

PRIEST. Frankly I'm not sure, but it's not worth the risk.

INSPECTOR. In that case I'll leave the matter in your hands, as there's no one here to represent Interpol.

PRIEST (*to* CHRIST). You've heard, I've been able to spare you some of the public disgrace. But now I must ask you to collect your things and go immediately. I can't risk your contaminating the young people we have here. I'm very disappointed in you. Oh, I'm not thinking of myself and all the wasted effort I've thrown away – but you've let yourself down. It's too late to say it now, but you weren't without promise – and you've thrown all that away. You'll regret it in a few years and you'll look back on this and see we were right. I hope by then you'll have learned something. You'll never make anything of yourself if you go on the way you've started. I shall say no more. (CHRIST *comes down from the cross and starts to leave. He stops when the* PRIEST *talks again.*) God knows what your family will think of this. You've got a good family and they gave you a start in life many others would envy – and you've let them down, too. I shan't go on. Please leave quietly. It's too late for explanations and apologies. It's past amends. There is some conduct that's too underhand to be put right. I've finished now. (CHRIST *leans against the cross in boredom.*) Why didn't you say if something was troubling you? You know you could always turn to me. I'm not a hard man, I'm fairly reasonable and open – I think I can say that. There's nothing more to be said. The whole thing is best left in silence. In fact I'm too upset to speak. (CHRIST *hangs one arm over the horizontal bar of the cross.*) I'd give you another chance if I thought it would help. But there's no point. I have to remember the others in my charge. It's not fair on others to allow someone like you to continue to be in a respectable institution like this. Go, and I hope you find somewhere where you can fit in. Have I made myself clear? (CHRIST *goes.*) It leaves a space. I shan't get used to a space up there. It seems wrong. The congregation expect something.

INSPECTOR. I'll help you out, padre.

> The INSPECTOR *gestures offstage. A young* POLICEMAN *comes on. He is dressed in a fascist-style uniform with an armband.*

Here we are, Kedgie. Here's a nice easy job for you. Stand up there on that wooden appliance. Up you get, lad.

PRIEST. Won't he find it tiring?

INSPECTOR. No. He's used to controlling traffic. He'll be all right if he puts his mind to it. You can do anything if you put your mind to it. Comfortable, Kedgie? Keep staring straight ahead, lad. Just think how they taught you to keep watch on the frontier. (*To* PRIEST.) That makes the place look tidier.

PRIEST. True, it's an improvement.

INSPECTOR. Didn't like the look of the other one. You can pick them out when you've had a few years in my job.

PRIEST. I sometimes had doubts myself. But he had such good references, so what can you –

INSPECTOR. You're looking fine, Kedgie. You'll be relieved in two hours, lad. Do you know what to do? We'll just have a little rehearsal. We don't want any slip ups. Church parade is a parade like any other parade. The same smartness and superior turnout and every movement at the double. (*Shouts order.*) Relief christ, to your post – *march*! (*A replica of* KEDGIE *marches in.*) Relief christ – *halt*! (*The* RELIEF CHRIST *halts in front of the cross.*) Old christ – descend – *cross*! Smartly, smartly, there! Stop waving your arms about you're not blessing the multitude now! Watch your step, eyes front, head up, don't look down or you'll fall through the water! By god, I'll make martyrs of the pair of you! (KEDGIE *has come down from the cross.*) Relief christ – wait for it, wait for it, don't anticipate the word of command – mount – *cross*! I don't want to see you move, I want to see you there! Get up that cross there! Halt! Put your arms out, put your arms out, lad! Don't stand there with your arms dangling, you look as though you're going to start playing with yourself! Wank in your own time, not the army's! (*Turns to* PADRE.) There we are, padre, now we're beginning to get somewhere, we're playing on our home ground.

PRIEST. I feel much safer. There's someone up there watching over me and I can trust and rely on him. (*Indicates bread and wine.*) It's a pity to waste all this. Would you like to take communion?

INSPECTOR. Oh I –

PRIEST. I've changed the wine.

INSPECTOR. In that case – it's a very civil thought of yours padre, and I'd be glad to oblige. Call on me any time.

    The INSPECTOR *kneels and the* PRIEST *offers him communion.*

(Curtain)

Poem: Bird

Fly on, bird
Over the winter city in ruins of snow
The beggar with broken wrists
The tanoi that learns speech

Fly on
Past men with heads for faces
In cars like snakes fleeing water
One book for rules and another for writing in

Fly on
Past time with a hatchet
The member washing blood from under his nails
The youth who says: I go along for the ride
And climbs on the gallows cart

Their glittering corn is deadlier than famine
Their water is dust and chokes cities
Sentimentality covers cynicism in their beds

Fly on, blackbird
With claw smashed through beak
Skull cracked
Wings like burned flags
Charred cracked firework
Fly on, fly on

Your hands give birth to children
And hold men waiting death
These are small things
If the sky is not lived in the earth dies

Story: Christ Wanders and Waits

Christ was condemned to walk on earth till men were no longer miserable. He wandered from place to place. Everywhere he found war, famine, imprisonment, plague, and people bleeding and crying for help. There was misery everywhere. Jesus asked every judge and general he met to tell him how to make men happy, but they didn't know how. After many, many hundreds of years he felt he couldn't bear any more of this misery. He'd heard of a wise woman who could do miracles and tell what would happen before it happened. So he went to find her.

He found her living alone, with a few pet animals, in an old house outside a town. The roof was falling in and the path to the door was muddy when it rained. The people in the town wanted to build her a new house near the centre of the town, but she wouldn't move. So they said, 'Perhaps it's as well. She's clever, but she's mad, too.'

Christ said to the old woman, 'I am condemned to live on earth until men are no longer miserable, but I find misery everywhere. Tell me why men are miserable and how I can make them happy.'

The old woman said, 'You ask very hard questions, Jesus. I'll think about it. Go away and come back tomorrow.'

So Christ went away. He decided to stay the night in town with a friend called Simon. When he got to the outskirts of town he saw a procession coming out of town, and one of the women in the procession was Simon's wife. When she saw Jesus she came up to him and said, 'Simon is dead and we are burying him.' Then still crying she caught up with the procession and went with it to the cemetery. Jesus went on into town. He wandered through the streets and then sat on a wall till it was morning. He was too tired to sleep. As soon as it was light he went back to the old woman.

He said, 'What is the answer?'

She said, 'Jesus, I have never been asked such hard questions. I can't tell you the answers. But I know where you can get them. We will ask someone who's lived all his life and can look back on it and understand everything that's happened to him. Now, I know many skills and I can bring the dead to life.' So she took him round to the side of the house where there wasn't much wind and she bent down and picked up a handful of dust and threw it in the air and it drifted into the shape of the dead Simon. Simon recognized Jesus and pressed his hand.

Jesus said to him, 'Why are men miserable and where can I find a happy man?'

Simon wept and said, 'I have lived all my life in this town and I hated it. My wife loved me but I made her unhappy. I've always been unhappy and I'm unhappy now I'm dead. There is nothing to tell you. I've learned nothing. What is there to learn? The dead mourn themselves and the living.'

The small wind blew and the dust floated away and Simon disappeared.

The old woman said, 'Shall I bring him back again, Jesus?'

Jesus said, 'No,' and went on his way. He wandered on for many more hundreds of years and one day he saw a bird in a tree. The bird had a worm in its mouth which it was taking to its chicks. Jesus said, 'I wish you could speak, bird. Then perhaps you could answer my riddles.'

The bird said, 'I can speak. So tell me your riddles and perhaps I will answer them.'

Jesus said, 'Why are men miserable and how can I make them happy?'

The bird said, 'Your riddles are very hard but let me think about them. I will tell them to my husband and perhaps he will know the answers.'

But then the worm in the bird's beak spoke. 'I can answer your riddles.'

The little bird was so startled at hearing the worm speak that it dropped the worm and flew away.

Jesus said to the worm, 'How can men stop being miserable?'

The worm said, 'Love one another.'

Jesus said, 'That is a new philosophy and I will go through the world and teach it. Now answer my second riddle. Where can I find a happy man?'

The worm said, 'The earth is my house yet you walk on it and use it as your own. I don't complain about it, friend, and when you die I welcome you into my house. We are very close together and I would like to help you. But how can I tell you where to find a happy man? Still, I will do what I can. You are very tired. Sit here and I will go round the world for you, preaching this new philosophy to every man I meet. And then I will tell him I am christ and ask him if he is happy – and when I come back I will tell you if I have been able to find such a man.'

So the little worm set out to crawl round the earth and Jesus sat down and waited.

Poem: Rest

The body falls
An X marking itself
Buries under its own weight
In its own shadow
Under the horizon in its narrowed eyes
It rests now

We wander from stretcher to table to fire
Faded like flowers and wire and cards
Using death rattles as slogans
Let it rest

The old bitch in her ivory tower
Makes trials of funerals
Calls dead to the stand
And swears virginity in body and mind

Remember it rests

I run quickly
Breathing on their breath
Sing in the argument
Dance with the strength of their stillness
They have taken away the rest
And I have received the lotus gun

Methuen's Modern Plays

EDITED BY JOHN CULLEN

	A Slight Ache and other plays
	The Collection and The Lover
	The Homecoming
	Tea Party and other plays
	Landscape and Science
Jean-Paul Sartre	*Crime Passionnel*
David Selbourne	*The Damned*
Boris Vian	*The Empire Builders*
Theatre Workshop and	
Charles Chilton	*Oh What a Lovely War*
Charles Wood	*'H'*

*   *   *

Methuen Playscripts

Paul Ableman	*Tests*
	Blue Comedy
Barry Bermange	*Nathan and Tabileth and Oldenberg*
John Bowen	*The Corsican Brothers*
Howard Brenton	*Revenge*
	Christie in Love and other plays
Henry Chapman	*You Won't Always Be On Top*
Peter Cheeseman (Ed.)	*The Knotty*
David Cregan	*Three Men For Colverton*
	Transcending and The Dancers
	The Houses By The Green
	Miniatures
Rosalyn Drexler	*The Investigation and Hot Buttered Roll*
Harrison, Melfi, Howard	*New Short Plays*
Duffy, Harrison, Owens	*New Short Plays : 2*

*   *   *

Methuen's Theatre Classics